No Fear Going Home after
Retreat, Treatment & Rehab

THE BEST татwо WEEKS OF YOUR LIFE

*After-Care Program Healing Anxiety,
Depression, Addiction & Trauma*

*3 books in One *Guidebook*Workbook* Interactive Recordings*

By
William Morgan

Copyright © 2025 by William Morgan

All rights reserved.

No part of this book may be reproduced, distributed, or transmitted in any form or by any means, including photocopying, recording, or other electronic or mechanical methods, without the prior written permission of the publisher, except in the case of brief quotations used in critical reviews or certain other noncommercial uses permitted by copyright law.

ISBN: 979-8-9987779-1-2

Walking Earth Printing

Walking_Earth@Outlook.com

Dedication

I humbly dedicate this book to my dear friend and teacher, Estelle Gerard, who founded the Lido Zen center in Florida, and has been a bright beacon for me and many others. She illuminated a path for me in my Zen practice and instruction. She introduced me to many of her teachers and influencers, including renowned figures such as Soen Nakagawa and Sheng Yen. Through her accounts, I felt a profound appreciation of their character and way of life as if I had known them personally. With deep gratitude I vow to repay her generous spirit forward to innumerable sentient beings.

Acknowledgements

I want to thank my many clients over the last 35 plus years. They trusted me in their lowest moments and inspired me to grow and learn. They nourish me in this life journey we walk together.

All my colleagues and clients at Holina Addiction and Trauma Center have been a great support these last years, especially the founder and friend, Yossi Zubari, who gave me the opportunity to participate in his vision.

Guo Go, (Jimmy Yu, PhD), Chan teacher and founder of the Tallahassee Chan Center and Dharma Relief in Tallahassee, Florida, has, with spare and deft guidance, strengthened my Buddhist practice when it was most needed.

Nathaniel Brandon was a great help and inspiration to me. He showed me the meaning of empathy and integrity, surpassing even his well-known intellectual capabilities.

I am deeply grateful to all health practioners dedicated to helping those in need and who have shared their wisdom through teaching, videos, and writings. Everyone builds upon everyone else's work to a great extent, and I am no exception.

Contents

1. Dedication 3
2. Acknowledgements 4
3. Introduction 11
4. Momentum Mastery 15
   The Horror of Returning Home 15
   Do I have to go home? 20
   Natural success abilities 21
   Your home treatment center. 22
   About this guidebook 25
5. The Five Horsemen. Noble Truth. 31
   The First Horseman: Focus. Mastering monkey mind. 33
       Focus is taking control.. 34
       Focus and thoughts 35
       Focus is much under misunderstood, underused. 36
       Principle of Maintaining Focus. 36
       Creating Deep Focus. 36
   The Second Horseman: Self-Awareness. First step for change 38
       Awareness grew at R/T and will at home. 38
       Awareness of what? 39
       How awareness is suppressed. 39
       Liberating repression, allowing awareness. 40
       Using greater awareness for better life 41
   The Third Horseman: Relaxation. In Perfect Tune 42
       Playing Beethoven on a Coconut 42
       Relaxation without a name 43

    The critical importance of Relaxation... 43

    Two relaxation procedures 44

    Barriers to relaxation... 46

    Relaxation. Sweet elixir 51

The Fourth Horseman: Action. Most underrated 52

    Retreat/ treatment letdown malaise inaction... 53

    Action experience. Thinking dream... 54

    Action from right intention, feeling grounded 55

    Fear of action 55

    Action is energy... 56

    How to take action (When you don't feel like it).. 56

The Fifth Horseman: Desire, rocket fuel of life. 57

    Your desire brought you to retreat/treatment. 58

    Connecting to powerful desire. 58

    Stop saying no to your desires. 59

    Let your true desire guide you. 60

6. Daily Program for Best Two Weeks of Your Life 61

    The Activities 62

    The Worksheets 64

    Daily 1 Plan Focus on Self 64

    DOWNLOAD AUDIO instructions/Meditations from free link: https://bit.ly/4iG4wQj
.... 66

    Instructions step by step for the Daily Plan... 66

    Big Breathing with Bell Procedure... 66

    Gate gate power chanting 5 minutes 66

    Mindfully walking with counting breath 67

    Stress reduction count breathing... 67

    Instruction. How to's reading.. 68

    Big breathing 3x power 68

    Mindfully Eating... 68

    Relaxation and confidence breathing procedure 69

    Gratitude energy meditation 69

    Gate gate 15 70

    Four position tongue release 70

    Daily 1 Review Spending time, Wasting time.. 71

    Instructions for Spending Time Wasting Time... 73

  Daily 1 Review: My Good Day Worksheet 74
  Daily 1 Review Vows for Tomorrow worksheet 76
  Daily Program days 2 through 14 78

7. **New life. Fresh thinking.** **131**
  Designed for success 132
  Breathing for happiness 134
  Breathing, power of survival. 135
  Toxic breathing 137
  Breathing as healing 138
  The 3 laws of emotion. 139
  Childhood Bugs and Malware 145
  Caterpillar and butterfly. 145
  Avoidance as tactic. 147
  Lost childhood, rediscovered self. 147
  Survival system 148
  Surviving childhood. Thriving adulthood 149
  Sensations, programming our childhood 149
  Childhood Stress Coping Mechanisms 151
  Love Intimacy. 151
  The Power of Silence 153
  Fear 156
  Play Beethoven on a coconut 157
  Damage Childhood, Broken Relationships 159
  Adult Relationships after Childhood 159
  Control is Repression and Avoidance 160
  How to Live with Damaged Childhood 162
  Why why why? 163
  Need for Perfection 168
  Letting go 169
  Dreaming and Envisioning 171
  Emptiness. 172
  Understanding Emotional Healing 173
  Not your fault 174
  Hanging on to the Past 174
  Knowing yourself 175
  Recognizing the True Self 176

Small, smaller, smallest 177

8. How To's for Living Life 179
How to breathe for liberation.. 179
How to strengthen focus. 180
How to quiet your thoughts. 181
How to let go of all life-numbing tension.. 182
How to chant. 184
How to comfort nervous system with vibration. 184
How to eat less for more flavor. 185
How to create purpose. 186
How to let yourself flow. 187
How to manage anger. 188
How to see reality 191
How to Build Confidence 192
How to Live with Damaged Childhood.. 194
How to live mindfully.. 196
Reading supplemental and video influencers. 198

Introduction

My intention for this guidebook is to significantly improve quality of life, especially after retreats and treatment. Retreat and treatment may include rehabs and detox programs, or therapeutic experiences targeting anxiety, trauma, or depression. Whatever the reason you left home to enroll in R/T, by following this program at home, you will quickly notice better health, increased productivity, and greater satisfaction. Your spiritual growth will also continue and deepen. With consistent effort, you will gain insights and benefits as others have who have followed this program.

I've designed this program to be so unique that it works for anyone desiring more from life. It doesn't matter one's intellect, background, or skill level, just follow the program and allow it to work on your human technology. I'm not a believer in typical self-help books that promise solutions to life's challenges but leave readers struggling long-term with the same issues. They offer cures, answers, charts, and diagrams, and by the last chapter, unveil a solution that typically involves "thinking better" or "behaving better" under certain conditions.

It's a Western mindset that all problems can be solved by applying the mind correctly. Yet the forces behind unhappiness and debilitating issues lie much deeper, beyond the reach of thought or willpower. Purely intellectual solutions signal that the root of the problem isn't understood, and thus, won't be solved. Real solutions aren't about playing the game of life better through refined thinking; they're about learning to live life as an art, flowing from a balanced emotional state.

Most problems originate from emotional conflict. This is a sensory issue first, and a cognitive one second. Thinking and behavioral changes alone won't bring long-term improvement because emotional forces always override them.

The activities and ideas in this guide are based on over 35 years of experience, fundamental human technology, and 2,600 years of Buddhist teachings. At the heart of this is experiential learning, understanding yourself through awareness-based experience. Experiential learning begins with emotion, and the mind simply follows. This program is guided by hands-on learning, experience, and reflection. It mirrors how we naturally learn most things in life, including how we develop our emotional attitudes.

A rational, self-help book, no matter how intellectually satisfying, cannot create true transformation. This program includes the essential element of non-thinking practices. Only through quiet stillness can thoughts become focused and meaningful. Anything less cannot deliver lasting well-being.

Improved thinking and better control may sound appealing, but they are mere sugar for the reader seeking long-term solutions. They bring fleeting enthusiasm and short-term results. While critical thinking is important, it fails without emotional stability. I refuse to leave the reader where they began, frustrated and believing the fault is theirs for not grasping the concepts. Many self-help experts blame the reader's intelligence, subtly suggesting that only the "smart ones" can succeed.

Here, I offer root-level solutions, not overexplained theories. The daily plan is based on becoming your intuitive, natural self, free from mental conditioning. Following this program is like going to a mind-body studio: well-being becomes unavoidable. While many can describe trauma, depression, and anxiety in great detail, such analysis does little. They advocate "understanding the issue" and changing behavior in response to it. I call this the "understanding-solution", and it's doomed.

If logic and determination truly solved personal problems, the success rates of retreats and treatment centers would skyrocket. But they haven't. Healing and happiness must originate from the non-thinking self. The programs we live by are emotionally driven. It's the damaged emotional program that must be repaired, not by thinking, but by reconnecting with our authentic self. Our thoughts, ironically, are often our greatest limitations.

Zen and Chan Buddhism reach the true understanding of self through experience, not theory. This approach has been known for millennia but remains underutilized in the West. Our original nature, calm, aware, and intuitive, is more powerful than intellect. It emerges when the mind is quiet. Deep down, we know that living a fulfilling life is more about being human than thinking like one. So how do we get there? How do we reconnect with the human inside? Start with the activities in the daily program.

The big questions remain: Why do people suffer? And how can happiness be achieved? The core answers lie in the sensory self which requires different strategies. Thinking as a primary method will always be insufficient. Thinking harder won't solve life's deep problems; any more than a bigger computer can fix its software. Humanity has become more knowledgeable but unhappiness and suffering persist. What Buddhists call right practice, the sensory focused approach, has been relieving pain and delivering happiness for centuries.

This program provides daily activities to connect with your emotional-sensory self. Interestingly, though there are many ideas here, you're not required to read any of them. When you're ready to start, go directly to Section Three and begin the program. No preparation is necessary. Profound benefits will evolve by following the activities and reflecting upon them. The workbook supports and encourages purposeful reflection.

As a Buddhist saying goes: A sword cannot cut itself. Neither can a distressed mind fix itself. For healing we must follow the right practices and activities. We must create space between the distressed and the true mind. This is the only true liberation from suffering. Have confidence that the solution you desire will emerge from your authentic self, discovered through moments of tranquility and clarity. New thinking is necessary and beneficial, with an emphasis on doing and experiencing without overanalyzing emotions. Higher consciousness can be achieved through non-thought activities. These activities align with the principle of human happiness and help sustain it.

The plan is flexible. Fit the structure into your day and adjust as needed. Keep the activities, rearrange them if necessary, but don't debate with yourself about doing or not doing them. Don't let old habits obstruct your new self. Having a schedule removes indecision and excuses. The few readings provided support the daily practices. Enlightenment exists in these daily experiences you are creating. New positive habits are being formed. Engage in practice, reflect on progress, and assimilate knowledge.

Koh Phangan 2025

Best 2 Weeks of Your Life

--- No Fear Going Home after Retreat, Treatment & Rehab

1

Momentum Mastery

The Horror of Returning Home

The one thing I hear most from my departing clients is about their fear and anxiety of going back home. The fear is they will lose their positive momentum from retreat/treatment. They've worked so hard to get to R/T, often sacrificed time and money, faced their worries and darkest feelings. It wasn't easy. Now, the dreadful moment is here. The time has come for them to face their problems head-on instead of escaping them.

I live and practice on one of the most beautiful islands in the world with many treatment centers and retreats. From a low point in their lives, people arrive with heavy hearts, broken lives, unhappy, and unfulfilled, yet hopeful and ready to tackle their problems. All over the world millions courageously set out to heal and change for the better. Change they do, but when it's time to leave a persistent terror arises, with horror at what might await them.

"I'm worried," they say.

"I'm afraid I'll fall back."

"I'm going to return to my old self, the self I came here to escape."

"Thinking about going home scares me."

Why? What is it about going home that provokes such fear?

Often, it sounds like this:

"I don't want to lose this positive feeling I have now."

"I don't trust myself. Maybe I'll revert to my old habits."

Confidence about going home is low.

"Maybe my new sense of happiness is an illusion, something that will disappear once I return to my old routine."

"I wasn't content with who I was before. I came here to renew myself, and I did, but I'm nervous my old patterns will resurface."

Every year, hundreds of billions of dollars are spent on retreats and treatment. People are suffering more and more, and many are desperate. Sadness and pain are everywhere. Quietly, all over the world, people leave their homes, families, and routines to begin a journey of healing, without any guarantee that it will work. Many are running from harmful habits and daily misery. Jobs lost. Relationships broken. A point of no return has been reached.

Maybe you know what I'm talking about. Maybe you are one of the many. Or possibly you didn't go to R/T, but you are tired of the life you have been living and desire liberation and transformation.

For some, this journey is a search for spiritual meaning. For others, it's a desperate attempt to rebuild a life. Most people are finally ready, after a long time, to commit to their own happiness. R/T may have been the first time in years, or ever, that they've taken steps to help themselves, to put themselves first. Their hope and optimism has been rewarded. But now, they are not so sure. After achieving so much in retreat or treatment, and finally feeling optimistic, the worry creeps in. Why? Because you're going home. A place where friends and family await. A place that should offer comfort, but instead, feels heavy with past pain and old struggles.

You're feeling thankful for your new view of life, and you don't want to lose it. Not now. Not after everything you've invested. Not when you're finally feeling human again. Exhilarated. Smiling. Laughing in ways you haven't in a long time. Life has meaning again. Naturally, you want to keep that, hang onto it however you can. But the desire to protect your peace is now complicated with fear.

Fear is completely normal. To fear what hurts you is healthy. The mind races to find strategies preventing living at home to destroy your peace and calm.

You start thinking of ways to delay going home.

"Can I take a side trip?"

"How much longer can I afford to stay away?"

"Maybe I could go to another retreat as a kind of halfway house?"

The anxiety bubbles up, spoiling what should be an excited return. You begin to doubt your healing experience.

"Am I really feeling better?"

"Did I learn anything?"

"Can I withstand the pressure of being home?"

"What am I doing, going back so soon?"

Other questions follow:

"Am I fooling myself thinking I've resolved anything?"

"I've failed before, what's different this time?"

"What will my friends think of this new version of me?"

"Do I really have the tools to handle them now?"

"Will home overwhelm me again?"

"Have I really changed?"

"I can't continue these treatments at home, was this a waste of time and money?"

These are all honest questions. But they're the wrong ones. They stir doubt. They feed fear. But they don't lead to solutions. This is your old program talking. Let's change that. To find peace and remove the fear of going home, you must do two things: Understand why you feel better right now. It may not be for the reason you think. What if it's not home, friends, and family? Those may stimulate you in the old ways, but you're old, habitual reactions do not have to remain. If you really understand why you're feeling better, you'll see that your reactions will be different. That you won't be stuck in the old routines.

The second thing you must do is create a simple, unshakable plan for living at home. It must be uncomplicated and require only small, consistent effort. Must give you structure so that you don't have to argue with your old self to do the things that you've learned to do for yourself. You have a plan to help yourself every day, throughout the day you have specific activities which make you feel better and maintain you're well-being.

If you go back to the same thinking and behavior you had before the retreat, nothing will change, will it? And if you don't have a new idea on how you're going to live your life and have a plan for living it at home, you'll return to the old lifestyle. The lifestyle you don't want, the lifestyle that you're afraid will put you back into that unhappy, unsatisfied self. This two week program is exactly what you need to avoid that situation.

You've heard the saying: You can't do the same thing and expect different results.

This program transforms your home life from the inside out. Your environment stays the same, but how you see and respond to it does not. You will be doing things differently, applying the best tools from R/T, and running a schedule designed around your best intentions. Home will never be the same again.

You've tapped into a sense of wellness during your retreat that you haven't felt in a long time. But here's the truth: it wasn't just the therapies and classes that made the difference, those can fade and are hard to duplicate.

What truly matters are the natural skills and abilities you used to attend sessions and classes, to contribute, to engage. Using the same qualities that brought you to the R/T in your life at home with continue to grow your wellbeing. You already possess them and have been using them, so let's keep them going. You probably didn't notice them since they're subtle, innate, and powerful. I'll show you what they are and why they worked for you in R/T because they are essential to fulfillment and lasting change. Most are widely recognized in Eastern teachings. But if you didn't know anything about them, just know that this program is built around them.

We're going to take the essence of your healing experience and grow it into something for greater happiness. This time going home won't be overwhelming or defeating. Instead, home will be a source of strength, a place of warmth, comfort, and purpose.

Of course, you need support going back, who wouldn't? You'll find it in "The Best Two Weeks of Your Life." Support and a how-to guide for making it a reality. Your old life, the one that led you to R/T in the first place, wasn't working. It wasn't supportive, nourishing, or helping you grow. That's why you picked up this book and started reading it. That alone says something powerful about you.

You're ready.

You have hope.

You believe in your possibility.

This guidebook and program is for you, to help you build the life you want and will never lose again.

Do I have to go home?

Sounds ridiculous, doesn't it, to hear yourself think, Must I go home?

Maybe I don't have to go back. Home was the problem, or at least, it's where all the problems seem to be.

But you're not the first, and you won't be the last, to think about not going home. Many people delay their return out of fear and a lack of confidence. Just imagining being home gives them a knot in the stomach.

Maybe I'll take a little side trip on my way home, one thinks.

What will my friends and family think if I don't return? Thoughts run wild.

Any possible excuse to delay or avoid the inevitable feels like a good idea. The dread of going home can be so overwhelming that we put it off until there's no other option left.

When you left home it may have felt like a prison. Maybe you felt compelled to break out, and treatment or retreat was the way out. You had to get away from home and everything it represented. That decision to give yourself space was a gift; one you gave to yourself. It may have saved you. Maybe it's the first time in a long time that you made a real effort to help yourself. And now, you're thinking, why should I go back to the place where I was miserable.

But here's what I've noticed.

Knowing what helped you during your retreat or treatment will empower you to recreate those great feelings when you return home. Instead of focusing on what you did, turn the focus on how you did it. Let's do that and eliminate all the reasons to worry. I promise you that a little understanding of these greater truths of self-help and a living program for practicing these truths will give you want you want. It won't take long to experience the benefits.

Keep in mind it's the practice of these basic truths, The Five Horsemen. How does one practice focus? I'll show you in the program. How does one use awareness? I'll show you and you'll experience greater awareness and self-knowledge as you do the activities. This is learning by doing. Feeling better by taking specific actions designed to repair your operating system and have you living your best life.

When people think about going home, they tend to focus on what they're doing rather than how they're doing it. They see themselves doing yoga, therapy, exercising, detoxing. They wonder, how can I possibly do all of this back home? How can I have classes and therapy while juggling work and family? This thinking has some truth to it. Fortunately, it's not the classes which are the primarily drivers of happiness and satisfaction.

It's easy to recall how in responsibilities, bills to pay, people dependent upon them seemed to drag them down. So they think, I can't just ignore everything and focus on myself like I did here. I don't know how to do this. But let me tell you: you don't have to fear it. Embrace the fear and think of it as an opportunity. On R/T you faced fears and grew. As the saying goes, 'the way out is through.' Sayings don't become sayings without some truth in them.

I'm sharing with you some of the secret tools I've learned from decades of working with people who desire personal empowerment. No obstacle can hinder your progress when the program's practices, activities and exercises are consistently followed.

You will soon start experiencing the clear and significant benefits.

Natural success abilities

As I said, the central reasons behind your success in R/T stem from what I call The Five Horsemen: focus, awareness, relaxation, action, and desire. These innate abilities were essential to your achievement. They are forces doing the heavy lifting for living well. Without them, life becomes a mental exercise, lacking depth and meaning. They empowered you in R/T, and they will continue to empower you at home. These five horsemen are among the most powerful skills for living fully.

You can strengthen and apply them to create a life unlike any you've known before. You've always carried these essential powers within you, and they're still there now. So why haven't they always been available to help you be your best?

There are two main reasons:

1. You were initially infected with a viral program that significantly reduced their power and effectiveness in living life well.
2. You were never taught how to develop and improve these abilities to maximize their potential.

The bugs and viruses of a stressful or traumatic childhood damaged these abilities, leading to long-term dysfunction. Although, because of this 'infection', one's internal program hasn't operated as it was meant to, to help you survive and thrive in a demanding world. It can be cleaned and restored to it's one hundred percent operational capacity. When it is, life becomes very easy.

The same process of cleaning and restoring will also enhance these abilities for empowering you to live in a new, authentic way. It's two for one: healing and thriving.

This guidebook is uniquely designed to support that journey. The activities and exercises here aim to restore you to your natural operational level. It's possible you haven't reached that level since early childhood. You may have never experienced life lived with all your abilities without obstacles. The activities with do the work for you subconsciously and organically as a result of your efforts.

Your home treatment center.

Think of going home as stepping into another kind of retreat. You're not leaving treatment, you're continuing it, just in a different environment. In fact, life is one big learning experiment. We're always changing and the world around us is always changing and we need to change with it. This can be described as an adaptation process. If we're changing and everything around us is changing then we need to be flexible and open-minded to grow with this change. Anything short of that and we will not be functioning at a very high level. We either accept that or we become burned out and declining. R/T was change and now home, which had become stale and stagnate, will be your life laboratory for change. Here you'll keep experimenting and discovering your best self. This is a continuation of your R/T growth.

Yes, you'll encounter situations and people who are tied to your past problems. But what's also true is that you're returning with a level of confidence and strength you didn't have before. You'll see these situations and people from a different point of view. Being more aware you'll be free to act positively for your best self. You're not losing what you learned and felt during R/T, you're bringing it all home with you. And you'll have this guidebook by your side.

Think of going home as a mirror, reflecting on how far you've come. Identify the areas that still need your focus. This is the process of self-learning and it is necessary for your continued growth. Embrace mistakes. You've lived a whole life without all of your abilities so you know you have behaviors and thoughts that weren't working for you. But now you will have greater awareness and understanding so you can make new choices to live the life you wish and not the life you were conditioned to live.

We often see home life as the source of our defeat. The pressure, the stress, the obligations, they feel relentless. But what if we flipped that perspective? Let's view everything that happens at home as an opportunity to express our new self. Recognize and try to free yourself of the obligations of the past. Let the opportunity of being home rise Above the obligations of home. The place won't change and the people are not going to change right away, if ever. Accepting that alone will Relieve a lot of that previous dysfunction. The one thing that has changed and the one thing you have control over is you and how you respond. It's good to know you are not dependent on the people or the place.

To achieve victory, seek it within yourself rather than from external sources. We don't control other people, but we can control our responses. Instead of constantly trying to manage or cope, let's begin to free our minds from habitual thinking by creating space between our endlessly spinning thoughts and our quiet, peaceful self. The program will guide you in doing this. No explanations. No judgments. No overthinking. Using intentional, conscious choices. This takes practice, and you'll get it through daily activities.

Letting go of those thinking patterns you were stuck in before you left is how to transform the home experience. When you realize you're having the same thoughts, you let them go and just focus upon the sights and sounds in front of you. You can make a decision about it later you don't have to react in the old ways. And we can go further than letting go of the patterns by letting go of thinking altogether. This is real liberation. It may sound very strange stop thinking, but this is fundamental 2 eastern practices for peace and happiness. This program uses and instructs a non-thinking, non-reactive approach.

Going home isn't about revisiting the past. A history of emotional pain or unhealthy behavior doesn't dictate your future. You are now, moving forward. Life is about creating new experiences. You are under no obligation to relive old memories. As has been said, memories are merely the residue of the past which gets stuck in the net of the present. Not of very good use for living now. Others may expect the same from you, but you don't have to expect the same from them or under obligation to give them what they expect. Living in the present is the art of living well.

By living in the present, you build your future moment by moment. We all have goals and dreams but we don't live them, we use them to inspire the present moment. Build your future moment by moment, day by day. That's what we're doing with this two week plan. We're creating a great future by living our best lives now. And this is true for your home life. Have confidence that you can live with greater satisfaction in your home life. Be prepared to overachieve in the very spaces where you once underperformed.

Approach this next phase, going home, with a beginner's mind and an optimistic view. You're not going back to your old life. You're going to familiar places and people to create something new. Open your eyes and ears wider than ever, just like you did when you arrived at R/T. Forget what you think you know.

Mark Twain, the American author, said something to the effect that it's what you know and think you're right about that causes more problems than what you don't know. Buddhists simply say let go of your thoughts.

Allow yourself to begin seeing the familiar in completely new ways. It's possible because it doesn't happen with your eyes and ears, and thoughts, but with your deep self, the quiet self, the true mind. In <u>The Best Two Weeks of Your Life Guide</u>, it will help you let go of your mind. You'll experience a shift in dominance from your thinking mind to your higher consciousness and intuitive intelligence. With this shift you'll avoid the pull of old destructive habits and patterns. You'll feel the joy and excitement that only comes when you're living with the wonder of a beginner and the wisdom of a old soul.

About this guidebook

The first two weeks back home can be both the most helpful and the most critical for restructuring your life. Those 14 days can launch you to new heights, or you can fall back into old habits and ideas. It's a choice rooted in desire.

The best approach is to hit the ground running with a solid plan and maintain the momentum gained from R/T. While this is especially powerful during those first two weeks, the truth is, you can use this guidebook at any point. You might return to it six months from now, or even six years, and still find something valuable. Each time you revisit it, the experience will feel different, because you will be different. That's the purpose of this plan: to offer ongoing support as your life continues to evolve.

The power of the daily plan is when you follow it, it won't allow you to fall back, because each day you're supporting yourself moving forward. It keeps you grounded and anchored in the present. You don't debate or negotiate with your old self's programming. You simply follow the schedule, a structure filled with proven activities. It is not your destiny to fall back into the habits you left behind, or to be overwhelmed by familiar pressures and problems. But it is your choice. Destiny is not shaped by reconstructing or focusing on your past. Let go of the desire to repeat or avoid what has already happened. Instead, focus on living your best present. Build your future through what you do right now—today.

Based on the Five Horsemen, the simple exercises and daily practices help cleanse the mental "bugs" and emotional "malware" that may have been embedded in your original self, even if that self never had a chance to thrive before. What emerges is your true nature: stronger, more confident, and filled with love. This is your birthright. This is the life you were meant to live before your body and mind were trained by fear, pain, and doubt. The goal is to restore that better version of yourself that has always been within you.

You don't have to read anything extensively, just follow the plan. Read what interests you when you need it. This guide emphasizes experiential learning, which is more transformative than academic input. It's about doing, reflecting, and feeling, drawing from your sensory and emotional experiences. Yes, we are thinking beings. We crave understanding. But restoration doesn't come from thought or reading alone. That approach only polishes the old thinking. We live life from our sensory-emotional self, then follows thinking, not the other way around.

This program is complete: mental, physical, and spiritual. The procedures and activities within it are designed to create beneficial experiences that go beyond mere thought and concept. The heart of it all lies in the daily plan in Section 3, which provides a structure so you don't need to overthink it. Simply do it. If needed, you can adapt to fit your personal schedule. What matters is maintaining a consistent routine for new, positive habits to replace the old, harmful ones.

Running this program will help you discover deeper meaning and purpose in your life. You require time to be kind to yourself, which the activities give you. The growth worksheets are reflective tools to help you observe, question, and value yourself. They guide quiet self-contemplation. In Section 3, you'll find a link to recordings of the procedures, making it easy for you to listen and learn for applying them. With use you'll feel increased confidence and satisfaction in your life.

There's a section of short discussions on myths and misunderstandings about life issues. If you're curious about any of the topics, it's there for you. Another section answers some of the important "how to" questions I'm frequently asked. There's no particular order, go to the index and see if something speaks to you. As you progress through the program, revisiting the same topic multiple times can reveal new and helpful insights.

The concepts in the "How to..." and "Fresh Thinking..." sections offer useful tools for breaking free from self-limiting beliefs. They'll help you "run the program" of life with greater clarity and understanding. But this is not yet liberation. Even the most brilliant ideas are like a house of cards when faced with physical tension, it will always dominate the mind.

Until your mind and body are truly liberated, the monkey mind remains in control. This program provides liberation from the 40,000 or more everyday thoughts controlling your life. Become the master of your mind and not the slave of it. You'll discover clarity, peace, and empowerment.

Freeing both body and mind requires going deep within and connecting with the pure, non-thinking self. We must learn how not to think, how to be silent and peaceful, in order to free ourselves for new possibilities. Only then will our thinking minds begin offering thoughts that deserve our attention.

The work-growth sheets give you objectivity, like a high-flying bird looking down from above.

What am I doing with my life?

What am I thinking when no one is listening?

What would I desire if self-love replaced fear?

Who am I beneath the roles I play each day?

If I could dream my best self, who would I be?

These sheets will help you discover meaning for your life. Incorporating them into your daily routine builds self-esteem, proving your commitment to self-care.

Your goal at R/T, to achieve personal growth and well-being, now enters its most profound and beneficial phase. Going home is the unavoidable and desirable next step in the transformational journey you began with R/T. This program accelerates that journey, offering a dependable vehicle for your path forward. It's equally scary and exciting.

You left home to come home again. Discover your way home, to the coordinates of happiness and contentment. Use this guidebook as your spiritual map, helping you stay on course through all the celestial and earthly storms you may face.

Here, you will find an awakening experience, one that extends far beyond the best two weeks of your life.

2

The Five Horsemen. Noble Truth.

The five horsemen are the noble truths of a life lived well. And it's the truth of your experience at R/T. These are the underlying, hidden strengths behind R/T, not on the schedule but powering all the therapies and activities . These truths are essential for the better self, for the full and contented life. They reveal one's deep self by raising consciousness. Their nobility lies in generating a life a purpose and meaning and creating spiritual value by living mindfully. Their truth is revealed only by experiencing them, becoming more aware, then reflecting and reorganizing ones view. They power everything good and beneficial in a human life. Yet they are often ignored and not given credit due for the healing and empowerment they bestow.

These underlying strengths improved during your R/T experience are more important than all the therapies, treatments, and classes you did. These five essential strengths are secrets simply because they are intuitive and undervalued. They weren't listed on the R/T schedule. They weren't in the brochure. They are difficult to quantify; how to you measure focus? But becoming aware of these five horsemen and learning how to grow and apply them, you create mental and emotional well-being. Those are the goals of this unique program.

These forces were at work beneath your activities at R/T and you didn't even know it. I call these powerful forces, The Five Horsemen. The Five Horsemen are the heart and soul of the exercises and activities this guide/workbook is created, *as they were the heart and soul of you R/T experience.* They are the foundation of all well-being. Without their foundation any healthy house you build will eventually collapse. These horsemen will be working for you as you follow this two-week plan. Of course, you can't recreate all those focused classes and self-improvement therapies when you go home, but you can continue to strengthen these hidden skills and improve your life. They were not a part of the program at R/T, but because of these you are stronger than you realize and are absolutely prepared for going home. The secret skills most benefiting treatment and retreat are the five horseman. They are the strongest forces in human nature.

When you know these hidden unseen forces you'll realize that you can keep your going at home and maintain your contentment. But not for the reasons you think..

The exercises and activities develop skills for living well because of these necessary building blocks. With each day you will become more confident and empowered to live your life the way you choose. This is how you will have the greatest 2 weeks of your life and beyond.

Why are you feeling so much better after retreat/treatment? Knowing why will give you more confidence for going home. It will help you create contentment and fulfillment. It's not because of the yoga classes. It is not because of the traditional and holistic therapies. It wasn't your healthy eating that changed things. It wasn't getting clean and detoxing. Yes, it was all of those things, but not exactly. It was so much more. Thinking that your new-self came about because of any of these things is the reason you're worried. These activities can't sustain you at home and you know it. First, you're not going to do them all and secondly, they are hard to duplicate. And thirdly, without the underlying abilities they are all form without deep benefit.

My five horsemen are the keys to creating the same frame of mind that served you so well in R/T. They are fundamental to peace, clarity, and happiness. Though well-known and respected in Eastern practices, they are often underestimated or overlooked in the West. What really happened in that yoga class beyond breathing and stretching? Are the self-realizations you heard in therapy setting you free or is there something else at play? Being clean and detoxing is a great step but how can one go back and maintain it? How's your fundamental human condition being improved by all these R/T therapies and activities?

Let's look not at the obvious of what you did but the unseen, the secret of you how did it. By recognizing what's working beneath all of your activities, you will see how easy it is for you to continue growing your recharged self. No worry about falling back into an unhappy, dissatisfied life. You can go home with confidence, without fear. This guide will show you exactly what you need to do based upon what really happened to make you feel better during R/T and keep it going for years to come.

The First Horseman: Focus. Mastering monkey mind.

Focus is the unseen horseman who played a huge role in your growth and well-being during R/T. While on R/T you improved your focus without much thought of how or why you were doing it. But in every therapy and class, you were directed to give attention to the activity. You were asked to look at this or concentrate on that. Your focusing ability improved and reached new levels of peace and self-satisfaction. Thus, during your time in R/T, you were enhancing your focus, resulting in improved well-being. In this two-week program we're going to create a deeper level of focus you may have never thought possible by using specific methods for developing highly skilled focus. Focus is what we use when we meditate for mindfulness. Focus is medicine for mind and body and home is the perfect place to keep it growing.

Without sustained concentration, we flutter like a butterfly from thought to thought. There's some interesting new research. Human brains absorb 10 billion bits of sensory data every second and yet can only process 10 bits. The assumption is that our brains operate in two modes at the same time: a receptive brain that takes in millions of bits of data and an inner brain that focuses on one small portion of that data at a time. Other research says we have 40,000 daily thoughts that are constantly spinning in our head. We don't need the research to know we've got a lot going on inside our heads and sometimes this is too much to handle. It's clear that without the ability to focus on one thought or idea, our lives can become chaotic. We need not only the ability to focus, most have this to some extent, but the ability to maintain focus under stress which is important. Recognizing and strengthening our focus, are essential for living our most productive lives.

Achieving the ability to focus at will presents a considerable challenge. Chronic tension, stress, and distracting habits keep us confused and out of touch with our own bodies. Concentrating allows us to reconnect with our inner selves, and the more intense our focus, the stronger our self-anchoring becomes. If there's one antidote to depression and anxiety it would be deep focus. Focus helps us stay calm and relaxed in any situation. To remain focused and not become overwhelmed during emotional insecurity requires strength of focus. This strength can be boosted following the daily plan. Deep focus helps us connect to our greater purpose and meaning stemming from our true nature of love and compassion. Developing focus is crucial for both recovery and success.

Focus is taking control.

We are slaves to our minds instead of masters of our thoughts. Our automatic responses to situations result from our minds being conditioned to react. Since childhood we have been told or shown how to respond to life situations. This conditioning has been imprinted upon our developing minds. People say, he/she made me do it, believing they had no choice. In certain situations, like when experiencing frustration, anger, or a sense of belittlement, we may believe there is only one appropriate way to respond. It's as if the sensory-emotional impulse its own natural reaction is part of a mathematical equation where $1 + 1 = 2$. One, if you do this or this happens, two, I will always react in this way. Their thoughts are telling them to react in a certain way and then justify the impulsive actions by saying *they* hurt me, *they* made me angry. *They* deserved what they got. And this reaction, these thoughts, are directly traceable to childhood. This is the opposite of control.

Focusing on the present gives us control to act in the most beneficial way and not react from habit. If we can't stay focused on the present reality, if our reactions have been set in childhood, how can we live effectively? Our thinking is our philosophy, our coping strategies for life. If our thought processes come from our past experience, how well can we cope in the present? The coping and defense strategies of a damaged childhood are sure to fail our adult. Developing stronger focus is the first step in transforming these self-defeating strategies.

By focusing on the moment, we can manage life easily without the confusing layers of childhood impulses. This is not difficult but requires practice and methods, as I've supplied in the daily plan. The child wasn't focusing, they were quickly reacting for their survival. It wasn't their fault; they did what was necessary. And now, after having been trained like any animal is trained to act to certain provocations, the ability to see and control current situations is obstructed.

Focus and thoughts

We are following our thoughts like monkeys jumping through the jungle of our mind. It's often called monkey mind because without focus there's little control or order. Buddha teaches that monkey mind is the source of most of our problems. Our thoughts, often just fleeting notions instilled and cultivated since childhood, hold little significance to our true self. Yet, we hold onto our thoughts as though they are the one and true source. We refuse to let go of what we know and what we tell ourselves, confusion and all, as if they are high truths given us from beyond. In accepting our thinking as the high court of life, we block ourselves from greater self-knowledge.

What if the source of our true nature lies deep within ourselves, far from our thinking and habitual ideas? Focus then becomes the tool to explore our deeper self, our true, essential self. We focus upon a sensory object, like breathing or sound or any object allowing our thoughts to fade quietly into the background. In this quiet self we have clarity, and freedom to live our best lives. Using specific focusing methods we can connect with true self. From this connected and anchored self, we can reach into our monkey mind to choose beneficial ideas from the billions bits of information and tens of thousands of thoughts. Behold, the monkey mind becomes useful. Strengthening focus for mastering our minds.

Focus is much under misunderstood, underused.

- **Focus cultivates being present**: Focus on sensory objects connects with our bodies and the present flowing moment. Now life is full.
- **Cultural appreciation of focus**: Western culture often undervalues focus compared to Eastern practices like Buddhism, which see it as crucial for spiritual practice.
- **Benefits of strong focus**: Manage stress, prevent confusion during emotional turbulence, and make life simple, and manageable.
- **Retreat and treatment impact**: During R/T, improved focus was achieved through clear goals and absence of home distractions.
- **Deep focus**: Maintaining prolonged attention to sensations without judging and awareness of spiritual presence, connects us to our true self.
- **Maintaining and nurturing focus**: Necessary for willpower and determination, aiding in overcoming harmful habits and supporting positive living.

Principle of Maintaining Focus

The principle of maintaining focus is that by sustaining our concentration, we can elevate ourselves to a higher level of consciousness. This involves achieving a state of mental quietude and physical stillness. Higher consciousness represents an awareness of self that transcends explanation or judgment, devoid of concepts or preconceived notions, even gender. In this elevated state, there is no distinction between self and the world; all entities are interconnected. For instance, songbirds and us breathing the same air and sharing the sun and moon. There is a shared presence with all things. In our highest consciousness we experience our essential spirit and inherent qualities beyond the confines of our mortal existence. Maintaining focus facilitates this profound consciousness of this, our true nature.

Creating Deep Focus

Focus is a basic part of our human technology. Similar to how gravity is an earthly force acting upon us wherever we are, when we apply focus, we gain emotional and mental clarity. It's a force of nature. When we maintain focus upon a sensory object for extended periods, without distractions, thinking, or judgement, we heal our emotional wounds, create inner peace and calm, and experience our true, loving nature. That's a lot of benefits from something so simple, especially when we feel our lives are so complex and stressful. Could it really be this simple?

Yes, its simplicity is why applying this principle has been called miraculous. Maintaining focus is one of these things that cannot be learned except by practicing. Deep focus is an experience beyond any idea. Reading about focus only gives you procedures and goals. The benefits cannot be forced or produced. Practicing object-focus means paying attention to a specific object within or outside ourselves. We then observe while connecting with that sensory experience.

It doesn't matter how often one is distracted because the strength comes from coming back to the object and maintaining this process. It is the nature of our mind and bodies to distract us. The technique is not to zone out or avoid anything, but merely choose a method of focus and allow other things run in the background without giving them any attention. When our monkey minds distract us with thoughts or irritations, we return to the object of focus.

Focusing away from our thoughts and concepts frees us from the heavy weight of thinking. It's as if we had been living our lives being blown through a tunnel, bouncing, and scraping our way along and then, through concentration alone, find ourselves free. Now the tunnel world in which we saw only a distant, dim light is now expanded, bright and clear. We sense ourselves as limitless as the universe.

Focus principle is used with the daily activities and recordings. You don't have to do anything to achieve the power of maintaining focus in your life except give yourself space and time for practice. It's best not to seek benefits but allow them to flow in their own way and form while you follow the daily plan. Life channels will open, creating more awareness as you maintain focus upon a sensory object. Consistently practicing focused meditation will help you connect with your true self.

The Second Horseman: Self-Awareness. First step for change

Awareness is a natural outcome of focus and concentration. The deeper the awareness the simpler it is, a quiet place where we stop talking and listening to ourselves. We stopped being the object and the center of our thoughts and we become the observer. When we concentrate deeply on an object, sensory-emotional pathways open, enhancing our awareness. Awareness connects us with our bodies and releases attachments to our thoughts and beliefs. As that process advances, we become more attuned to our sensory-emotional flow. Pure awareness allows us to perceive our genuine feelings and experiences without engaging in the habitual mental patterns we impose on ourselves and our view of the world. Sustained concentration further deepens our awareness, revealing fresh insights. Without the weight of predetermined ideas, we observe true reality, representing the essential truth of our being, which is more profound than the concepts and beliefs we have traditionally held.

Change and self-discovery start with expanding awareness. Deep awareness addresses avoidance, repressive strategies, and harmful emotional defenses. Self-awareness is crucial for well-being and happiness. Many people are only superficially aware and lack skills to enhance or utilize their awareness. Expanding awareness provides more information, pleasure, and satisfaction in life. Are we fully utilizing our awareness to enrich our lives?

Awareness grew at R/T and will at home.

You were naturally more aware coming to R/T. It was all new, trying new things with new people. You didn't have to be anything to anyone, you could take off your masks, free to experience everything you chose to do, open to trying something new. In Buddhism, this is called beginner's mind. With beginner's mind you were more aware and emotionally accessible than when you're at home. Aware, with a less rigid mind, you were ready to explore this new wilderness called you.

How do you bring beginners mind home when everything is totally familiar? How to prevent the old defenses and influences from taking over.? This is the task before us and why we have the daily plan to guarantee your continued success. Home will be your laboratory for developing and maintaining awareness skill is necessary. There's no better place to learn. It involves maintaining awareness of your body continuously throughout the day. Maintaining awareness without allowing your thoughts to dominate the present situation. It's a lot easier than it sounds when you follow the plan. Here you have the tools and practices needed to increase your skill and grow your contentment and satisfaction.

Awareness of what?

We are aware but not as aware as we can and should be. You are aware of sitting and reading and the room that you're in right now. You're aware of the ideas and thoughts. But in what way are you aware of your body? If we're not aware of our body we're not connected to ourselves. When we're not aware and connected to our emotional-sensory flow, which is the source of how we think and react to life, it's not possible to live fully. First, without awareness to our body's sensory-emotional stream, we don't have all the information necessary and available to us. Compare that to having a great computer program but not putting in enough information that it can function as designed. Second, by dwelling in our thinking mind, we deny ourselves the emotional richness of life. In our minds we are constantly judging, explaining, or justifying ourselves blocking us from our bodies and the pleasure inherent in living.

How awareness is suppressed.

Primarily we've developed awareness avoidance defenses to minimize discomfort and pain. These defenses usually begin early in a dysfunctional and upsetting childhood. As the final defense strategy for emotional survival, we shut down our awareness. Needing to resolve the agonizing the fear and the pain from our environment, we tense our bodies. Using tension to block awareness of sensations-emotions is the natural method. When physically trapped, as children are, the only escape remaining is emotional. The body's most powerful function to cope with emotional distress is breathing. Unfortunately, this learned defense creates emotional disorders for the grown up. Now as adults, every time a breath is taken, childhood awareness avoidance and minimizing strategies are revived, along with the underlying sensations-emotions.

Increasing this awareness problem is the fact we don't just shut down disturbing emotions when we use awareness avoidance tension, we minimize all our sensation-emotions. Joy, bliss, and excitement are minimized along with our fear and pain. As adults, we feel empty and hollow. We're not able to feel deeply and experience the fullness of life. Nothing is satisfying for long. The pain and fear of childhood has not been resolved with awareness avoidance, merely buried. Now the adult, in the absence of contentment and satisfaction, develops additional coping strategies: self-sabotage, addiction, depression, trauma, and physical disorders. Restoring sensation- emotional awareness is the only lasting solution for healing and for thriving.

Liberating repression, allowing awareness.

How do we break a lifetime of awareness repression? As we've seen, the process of awareness repression begin with persistent sensations, underlying all were the most intense sensation-emotions of fear and pain. It's obvious we're not going to open our awareness two sensations- emotions with a mental process. This all happened in childhood through sensations and involuntary responses. We need to use experiential methods that involve sensations. Only sensations can affect subconscious impulses, thinking never will.

This sounds like a daunting task, but it really isn't. We have control of one of those subconscious bodily systems that was used to repress sensory-emotional awareness. We have the breath. By focusing on our breathing, we are aware and have control of our repression. Learning to breathe fully and fluidly frees long blocked sensory-emotional flow.

Breathing normally and optimally actually reprograms our emotional state. Instead of sad and pessimistic we become happier and optimistic. Instead of anger exploding into rage and sadness dissolving into depression, sensory-emotions flow, rising and falling from 1 moment to the next. Nothing becomes stuck. We are unblocked. Remember tension is the mechanism and breathing is the form used by the subconscious. We can also consciously control our breathing. By releasing tension in the breathing system and restoring its relaxed natural response to sensations-emotions, we expand our awareness and restore our natural emotional state.

To create deep awareness, it is important to learn to breathe fully and fluidly as nature intended. Liberating the breathing instrument under all conditions maintains our awareness and physical connection. We focus upon our breathing, creating awareness. Maintaining focus for longer periods promotes deeper awareness. Awareness opens the sensory- emotional channels giving a richer life experience. As sensations flow, they dissolve and heal, allowing other sensations to rise in this continuous stream. The child couldn't allow healing sensory flow because of its intense pain and no freedom to heal. Their wound was always open. Our adult self in not trapped, can allow healing without fear. Focusing and maintaining awareness of the breath under stress is the ultimate goal for effective sensory-emotional processing. This approach can reset the breathing pattern and help address harmful and discouraging impulses and responses.

Practicing awareness is not going to reset the breathing instrument in one session any more than you'll develop strength in one visit to the gym. This is the mental studio, and it needs to be visited regularly. Think of it this way. If someone has been repressing emotions all their life, whether they're 20 years old or 60, this deeply rooted repression is in everything they do. It seems to me like a runaway train. We're not going to stop a lifetime of momentum in a moment. But with strong and frequent practice as is laid out in the daily plan, you will start to see benefits within the first week. Little by little drop by drop the harmful physical patterns will change, followed by the emotional and mental state. And there is no better or faster way to transform the awareness repression of childhood than with practicing awareness.

Using greater awareness for better life

We use awareness to see the reality of life. When we can see things as they truly are, life becomes much simpler. With our big brains and our 40,000 thoughts we are constantly telling ourselves what we've been led to believe. Reality's truth is buried under layers of culture and conditioning. Ninety percent of our ideas about life are just that, ideas. When we take the blindfold of labels and cultural ideas off, we see most of our problems we create in our head. Greater awareness reveals the greater truth. What is a tree if we didn't need to describe it? Who are we without our story? Shakespeare said "A rose by any other name would smell as sweet" what is our essence? Labels are the problem; the truth is in our sensations. As we focus upon awareness of our perceptions and sensations, labels fall away and our lives become richer and fuller.

Developing deeper awareness is like opening a faucet. Water (sensations and feelings) flows. Awareness is opening the valve to the reinvigorating water. Awareness makes no judgements, no comparisons, and requires no explanation or comparison. Practicing awareness, we realize that fear and courage, and pain and joy flow side by side. The sun is the sun, and the wind is the wind without explanation or mistakes. They belong to us and our only duty is to observe them. There is no bottom, no edge to awareness. Life, in its fullness, has no beginning or ending a long as we are awake and aware.

The Third Horseman: Relaxation. In Perfect Tune

Playing Beethoven on a Coconut

You have a unique and special melody within. It comes from within your true self. It is music from your inborn purpose and gives life meaning. Deep within us we have this flawless, brilliant melody, meant to be performed, to be lived. We may call it, 'My True Personality," or "My Best Self' but it is much deeper. This music we were born to play before early conditioning and events got in the way. It is yours and yours alone. Yet, you might wonder why you can't hear your melody or know your life's true meaning.

Think of your body as a stringed instrument like a guitar or violin. When our beautiful music is played upon a relaxed human instrument all our sensations and feelings are flowing. If your body instrument is stressed, if the strings are too tight, it will not be in tune. It will not play harmoniously with your life. Your music will be weak and harsh, very disturbing. Trying to find your purpose and play your special melody on such a tight instrument is like trying to play Beethoven on a coconut. Even his beautiful composition would sound terrible, wouldn't it?

Let's tune your instrument-body. Let's repair it and balance the strings not tight or loose. This tuning requires deep relaxation, awareness and focus. Restoring ones authentic relaxed instrument empowers expression of your unique composition. You will hear the meaning of your life and play it with purpose and passion. Keeping your instrument relaxed and well-tuned enables living in harmony with your true purpose, following your music.

Relaxation without a name

Relaxation was one of those underlying forces contributing to the growth experience you had in R/T. You got away from home, away from your obligations and all of your stress so you were definitely more relaxed. Don't underestimate the power it gave to your better feeling now. It was huge. You are familiar with this relaxation. All our best moments in life came when we were most relaxed. Birthdays, romance, vacations and, even your time at R/T. And now the worry for returning creates stress and tension about your old home life. We can find relaxation for you there would agree you've never known. But let's find something long-lasting at home no matter the worries or obligations big and small. Let's find the healing, refreshing relaxation level you may have never known. This relaxation cannot be named, only experienced. It is our original self-relaxation state.

Few people know how to relax. The commonly taught relaxation techniques can be beneficial but are often superficial. Superficial relaxation of the human body can relieve exhausting tension, but it doesn't maintain itself under emotional stress. Teaching the body to relax is not enough because it doesn't connect to one's energy channels (chi). Additionally, relaxation involves both physical and emotional components and both must be addressed to be maintained under stress, because relaxation is both physical and emotional. When we train the mind to relax, we relieve both the physical and emotional.

The critical importance of Relaxation

Relaxation is a natural state of being, yet people find it difficult to achieve. Life keeps us preoccupied with basic necessities and superficial gratifications. This was true in the less demanding time 2600 years ago when the wise Buddha observed that even those working humbly behind plows were caught in their spinning thoughts. People even then were disconnected from their true selves, questioning their lives. Buddha's teaching was to spend quiet, relaxed time with one's non-thinking, less attached self. This teaching is more relevant today than ever.

The natural state of relaxation promotes satisfaction and contentment. Oddly, it is a condition that we rarely experience. We are gripped by tension, feeling dissatisfied and unfulfilled. When tension supersedes relaxation, our performance diminishes, limiting both our talents and our ability to enjoy life. Operating at our highest and best is impossible without the fundamental physical and mental freedom that relaxation provides.

Two relaxation procedures

Relaxation is often compared to breathing, as people believe they understand it, but few actually do. Similar to breathing, there is a common confusion between the concept and the actual experience. Relaxation cannot be fully understood without genuinely experiencing it. There are two kinds of relaxation experiences, one you may be familiar with and one not. The most common experience is physical relaxation where you work directly on the body, stretching, massaging, or manipulating. This relieves physical discomfort and aids in injury recovery by relaxing muscles and soft tissues through external techniques.

The other experience is relaxing from within. For this the mind is relaxed to effect deep relaxation in the body by opening and connecting life channels, chakras, energy meridians and the like. This method uses objects for focusing the mind and deepening concentration. Relaxation from the mind to effect physical relaxations creates long-lasting inner peace and harmony. It promotes self-awareness that doesn't diminish under the most intense life problems. Both of these methods are tremendously useful and healing.

Physical, working from the outside

This is relaxation we know. It's vacations or downtime often spent like a zoo animal in a tree jumping around laughing and shouting trying to find a moment of release. Yet release eludes us. Tension has us in its grip, and on some level we're aware of it but we can't seemed to shake it. It's become our normal state revealing itself in behavior both small and large. We may have nervous ticks we can't get rid of. We may eat too much trying to relax and enjoy ourselves. We take vacations, go to events, sign up for classes all in an effort to find peace within relaxation. Some work some don't some work a little bit. It's never a waste of time learning to be a mechanic for our own relaxation, whether it be the practices of yoga, meditation, are direct methods for muscular relief.

Spiritual, working from the inside out

Buddha taught that a focused mind has no tension, is completely relaxed. What does this mean, focused mind? A focused mind has let go of all the thinking and ideas attracting our attention day and night. It's a quiet place where talking and thinking stops and words have no meaning, because there's a deeper meaning within the silence. Within the silence we find awareness of our true self. As we focus, our relaxation releases our body and mind. We fall into the deepest and quiet parts of ourselves. This is when our physical relaxation is transcended to spiritual relaxation so deep there are no words for it. It is relaxation without a name, and it is total.

There are degrees along this path. This type of focus and relaxation requires skill and frequent practice. But as we develop our practice, we find amazing realizations. Problems and confusion float away. Mental clarity comes with solutions and a new view of life. Childhood tension within our breathing system releases. We become less critical and angry, and our natural state of love rises above all to influence new thinking. Until then our thinking is our master. Now, our original self takes control. Our sensations-emotions rise and fall with just the right amount of weight and value they deserve and no more. We find we are living in the moment, on the razor's edge of the ever-changing present.

This is why we want to spend our time well, abiding in stillness, connecting to our authentic self. In doing this stillness practice, we set our intention to go where relaxation has no name and no words our descriptions. This healing space where our bodies and minds harmonize with the music of our purposeful self, music we were born to play. This is the reason there is a balance in the daily plan between experiential and conceptual activities.

Barriers to relaxation

Society

We live in societies where the emphasis is on pushing ourselves to exhaustion.

Working long days, multiple jobs, always thinking about getting ahead and attaining success and achievement. What's our next move, our plan? Always thinking. How to create the best impression, build alliances and make contacts that will further us and our quest to achieve and triumph. We are like mice and the wheels spinning, not knowing where we're going and not being able to stop. The only ambition worth chasing is meaning and happiness, and these lie within if we can let go.

When we look for relaxation, it appears to us as an event or happening. We want to go someplace and do something: big vacations, see important places, run marathons. We can't relax with a meal without taking pictures and at once sending them into the digital sphere. Our social media is filled with drama and our entertainment packed with AI un-reality. If we don't document our lives, our value diminishes, we don't exist. Unless we have a stream of pixels flowing into space and thousands of two-dimensional likes who are we? Gone are the days of family picnics and quiet times, taking walks to nowhere with all the time needed to arrive. Today, relaxation needs a drink, an exotic feast, and a spectacular. There must be celebrities and gossip to relax and enjoy.

Childhood repressive tension

Chronic childhood tension is the biggest obstacle to relaxation and the freedom it brings to our life. Childhood can be a trap or a time of joyful freedom depending upon the amount of comfort and attachment received. Trapped, an afraid animal in a trap doesn't express feelings, neither does the child. Because the because the child's trap was endless, the fear was constant.

Children yearning to create the feeling of safety, use tension to repress disturbing emotional sensations. This creates a false sense of safety which is never resolved in the child or in the adult.

This is how chronic tension develops and stays with you day and night. It is this tension that keeps you attached to your worst childhood feelings. This everyday tension now has trapped the childhood emotional state within you. The relaxation release is needed to transform this damaged childhood into a healthy restored adult operating system. Deep relaxation methods release sensory-emotional repression, restoring a sense of security and peace. Unstick emotions and allow them to flow using relaxation release procedures provided.

Guilt and relaxation

Many people in this modern, striving society feel guilty when they slow down. They feel like they're not doing enough for themselves, for their family, or for their communities. Along with this feeling comes the idea that there's never enough time. They have to be the first ones that worked and the last ones to leave. They're trying to live up to Those modern sayings, work hard play hard or the early bird gets the worm. But the problem goes much deeper. Not giving themselves time to relax is only one of many things they can't give themselves.

In an impaired childhood, guilt was the normal feeling. The child was always on alert, always in a hyper state of readiness for hiding or defending themselves. Always playing defense, never knowing what to expect or from where the next emotional blow was coming from. Questioning themselves as in what did I do wrong, now, or how do I protect myself? They never feel comfortable or safe. They are awash in feelings of guilt regardless of the fact they hadn't done anything. They are always on trial, requiring that they vindicate themselves, proving that they haven't done anything. Night and day they have to justify, or stand ready to, their very existence on this earth.

This child, now grown, cannot relax. The feeling of guilt is with them always but when they try to relax it becomes overwhelming. Relaxation opens the memories of their childhood surroundings and all the associated sensation-emotions. Even as adults they continue justifying themselves with every action, every relationship, and every breath. They're living the rule that they have been taught, that they're no good unless they're doing something. Staying busy is their slogan-philosophy hiding the truth that they don't feel worthy, and, if they pause their busy life for one minute, this depressing fact will be visible to all. With this deeply imprinted, their whole life is about proving themselves. They take pride in not relaxing. They work too much, worry too much, eat too much, drink and use too much, and do everything over the top. When you teach them how to relax, they don't do it because they don't want to feel all those gut-wrenching emotions from childhood. They become anxious, depressed, or addictive because they feel guilty to give their bodies and mind space and time to relax.

Tension. Emotional auto-pilot

Releasing tension in the body 24 hours seven days a week turns off the emotional auto-pilot tension has imprinted on body. Relaxing only tension, without trying to change how one thinks or act will change a life forever. Thinking differently and behaving better will be changed when tension is released. But until 1 is free from the emotional autopilot of tension there's no willpower great enough to overcome old habits of thought and action when under stress. Relaxation turns off this harmful emotional autopilot.

Emotional repression is a defense system that takes hold of us physically. Our emotional state becomes imprinted upon our breathing and body. Sculpted by our childhood emotional state, this sculpted form becomes our emotional reality. We might move like an animated sculpture, our movements projecting insecurity. Our posture itself signals we are carrying the weight of the world upon our shoulders and expect little from our life. We are the insecure man or woman moving with their stomachs pulled in and their chests out, marching along, trying to imitate an appearance of worth and self-love. Or we're, the quiet, head-down individual whose posture displays they do not expect much from others, and that life is a heavy burden where nothing comes easily.

It is important to understand how your body functions under stress and tension. Your body can trap you in an emotional state, keeping emotions on auto-pilot in a state of sadness, anger, or fear. By releasing physical tension and relaxing, negative emotions decrease, allowing positive emotions to surface. Notice how worrying about going home increases tension? Tension underlies worry and fear and fuels it. Releasing tension while maintaining relaxation despite stress or worry will improve your emotional state. This practice involves maintaining relaxation regardless of stress or chaos, leading to optimism, confidence, and control. Focusing on mental relaxation, the gloomy autopilot disengages, allowing your natural, positive emotions, happiness, confidence, and excitement to emerge.

Releasing tension and maintaining your relaxed state under the stress and worry of going home will improve your emotional state more than any one thing. Notice how the worry of going home produces more tension? Chronic tension runs beneath worry and fear and fuels it. The art of relaxation is maintaining it no matter the level of stress or chaos. As we release tension, we find power where there was weakness before, because tension is weakening. Become aware of the tension auto-pilot and apply the procedures in the plan. Turn it off and watch your new emotional state turn on.

Tension, life killer.

1. Relaxation is the solution to the killer of life, tension. Physical relaxation solves the majority of emotional problems rooted in early repressive tension from emotional conditioning. What was the last survival effort of the child is, ironically, now killing the adults ability to survive. Repressing emotions is not an effective way of living as an adult. In fact, it's a poor imitation of living because emotional tension puts all of life's tasks in the thinking mind. In this state one can function to some degree but cannot live with the richness and beauty of life.

2. Like carrying a piano around on your back, tension is exhausting and defeating. Your human system can only work at its best when relaxed. Most people are aware of this on some level but have no idea how severely it's destroying their lives. They don't know how to release and maintain that relaxed feeling. Tension keeps you stuck where relaxation allows everything to flow. With flow you heal from grief and trauma.

When you release tension for twenty-four hours, seven days a week, life changes forever.

- From harmful habits such as overeating, alcohol and substance abuse, and smoking, to overworking and engaging in excessive sexual activity, humans try anything to relax. Activities viewed as leisure, such as sports, vacations, shopping, or dining, are driven by the necessity to relieve stress. These temporarily calm the surface but underneath lies the storm. Breaking free from habitual impulses and living fully in each moment starts with a deep relaxation routine like here in *Your Best Two Weeks.*.

- Tension leads to poor decisions and detrimental life choices. It weakens us and diminishes our vitality. Tension suppresses emotions and perceptions, dulling the five senses and giving a diminished experience of life. Alleviating tension allows for a more relaxed state that's essential for overcoming anxiety, fear, and depression.

- Tension serves as a natural emotional defense mechanism. For example, we tense our arm to mitigate pain during an injection, brace ourselves when a broken bone is being set, and react physically in a dentist's chair to avoid pain and fear. Children often use tension as a primary coping mechanism against neglect and abuse. This results in the child developing lifelong tension-defense mechanisms that persist into adulthood. Unless this tension-defense is released, adults will continue to experience the negative effects of their childhood coping strategies, effectively living in a constant state of suppressed emotion.

- Tension acts as a protective shield against overwhelming emotions. However, this defensive shield is particularly harmful in the developing child. This defense becomes toxic and self-limiting. This is where deep relaxation techniques come into use. Using mindful methods for focusing and concentrating, we open life channels, heal and nurture a state of inner peace.

Relaxation. Sweet elixir

Relaxation Is the sweet elixir of life. It allows us to flow harmoniously with life. When relaxation is hindered by tension, harmony is upset, resulting in unhappiness and conflict. To achieve lasting transformation for your life, learn to be your best relaxation mechanic, fix yourself. You do this within the daily plan. What you're doing is restoring your natural state which was disrupted by your early situational surroundings. If you only do one thing for your mind body and spirit, relax.

Imagine responding to people and events calmly and confidently, instead of defensively and on edge. Imagine relaxing under stress, expecting the best outcome. The exercises and activities in this plan guide you towards the most calm and relaxed state you've ever been in your life. Learning to release and maintain relaxation is the greatest skill one can have for a happy life. Relaxation leads to control over your life.

Intellect will not overcome chronic tension. Why do you believe you haven't been able to think your way out of depression or anxiety or addictive behaviors? Because it is the nature of breath-body tension to overcome thinking. You must free yourself before you can effectively think clearly with purpose and meaning. With tension the old problems and worries agitate and weigh upon you. How well can anyone function with an elephant on your back? This is what chronic tension does to you. Simple life tasks become difficult. It's almost impossible to operate consistently at your best. And it's exhausting.

People are always saying, just relax. Others will say I know how to relax but it doesn't work. We know it's beneficial but are unsure of what we are looking for. It comes not from doing but by being. The relaxation we desire is not controlled by thinking but by freeing ourselves from thinking. It's non-think relaxation. It is practiced with conscious focus like in the breathing procedures here in the plan. It is experienced when we are our deepest, most quiet self, embracing the fluid moment. Future and past, where our worries and fear reside, have no presence here. It is a blissful, exhilarating being state which justifies the gentle, focused effort required. The relaxation route leading to this magical territory is ancient, as old as human technology itself. To arrive it requires the two magic potions, concentration and silence. With these skills showing the way, your original music will be restored and soar as it was meant to be.

The activities outlined in this guide are designed to alleviate both physical and mental tension. These methods have been proven effective and actively practicing them will help you achieve a profound state of peace. Simply reading about these techniques cannot substitute for the experience of implementing them. Now is an ideal time to begin, whether you are returning home or have already arrived. You can expect empowering results.

Partial relaxation is not sufficient for true liberation from chronic tension; we must seek complete relaxation. This extends beyond ordinary relaxation and requires delving deeply into sensory-emotional experiences. This two-week progression is crafted to engage both conscious and subconscious levels. Progress towards a profoundly relaxed state is inevitable. You will notice improvements in your well-being, feel lighter, and adopt a more positive outlook on life.

The Fourth Horseman: Action. Most underrated

Action creates experience and experience is the heart and soul of life. Have you noticed that doing things makes you feel better and, as you feel better, you do more? Simple concept, underrated. This is why you're feeling so good now after R/T. From the moment you started your booking through all of your experiences you were doing things for yourself. You're living your life, not just thinking about it. You were acting with the intent of being a better you. Intention, though powerful, is nothing without the force of action. Until then you haven't changed anything. Ninety percent of the improvement experienced on R/T can be attributed to the process of you taking action.

You can't wonder why I am not feeling as good as I did on retreat if you go home, sit and isolate yourself. Stop thinking about it and keep the action going. Some say to themselves, it's not working, I don't feel better now. Truth is they stopped doing things for themselves, stopped acting for their best self. Don't let this happen to you.

Action energizes the best of you. Remember, as soon as you left home, before you had one therapy or class, you were already felt better because of the action you took. You were hopeful. You believed you could. You had the intention of being a better you. Feeling good and happy resulted from acting, not by sitting at home thinking about it.

As in R/T the intention for this guide is for you to live your best self. Everything within, especially the daily activities, is designed for you to act and liberate your best self, to soar in life.. We emphasize the key benefits of R/T, creating new positive habits for living your life. The heart of this is an action plan; things to do, people to talk to, places to go

Retreat/ treatment letdown malaise inaction

At R/T you didn't think your way to feeling better although you may have had therapies which involved talking and thinking and new realizations. Helpful But they weren't experiences, except in the fact that you were sitting there with the intention of helping yourself. Actions create experiences. Actions flow from intention and motivation but without action these are very weak. Action adds spine and flesh to empty thoughts, no matter how noble.

The first action you took was getting on a plane or car or however you arrived. You had hours to sit with your new positive mental state on your way. You were going to help yourself find more meaning and peace. Even before that, weeks before that, you booked and planned your treatment. Starting then you were transitioning to a more positive state of mind. This cannot be overestimated. The trick is to how do we keep this positive state of mind at home. I'll show you.

Acting deliberately can be difficult if you're not in the habit of helping yourself or if you don't think you deserving of help. When you act your mental energize is positive. During R/T, you developed a positive attitude towards self-care, which became stronger with each action you took. You made a thinking choice, yes, but you then took action. Without action your better overall feeling would not have happened. You don't get well by reading a book. You don't get happy by watching a YouTube video. You get well by taking action. Any small positive action will greatly reward you.

Action experience. Thinking dream

Don't just dream, show your plan: "In five years, I want to be at the top of this or that." Every small step you take and every person you talk to should lead you towards that goal. Stop dreaming and start demonstrating your dream with small direct actions. A dream is merely an unconscious thought. A thought doesn't have the weight of a feather until you add action to it. There was never a eulogy spoken about all the great thinking the dead had thought. *But many are praised for the effort they applied and achieved through their actions. No matter how big or small, what was done is how they are remembered, and most importantly, this is the entire substance of their life.*

A dream or conscious thought has no weight and value of its own only what significance we give it. And how do we give it significance or importance? With another thought. Oh, that's a good idea, I should do that. And that thought also is weightless and so one thought is supported by another thought, and another, and so on, all which are transitory, rising and falling in the thin air of our monkey minds. That is until we give it weight with purposeful actions.

Give every action you take during the day the purpose and meaning of your dream. This could involve striving to be your best self, whether that means being generous, happy, compassionate, athletic, or any other positive trait. Ensure every action aligns with your dream. Every contact, bite of food, sip of a drink, and word spoken should reflect this purpose. By consistently aiming to be your best self, each step you take will be meaningful and aligned with your intentions.

Whatever your big dream is, dream for the future by taking small actions in the present. If you want to be the best singer, begin with one perfect note now, or golfer, taking pride in one good swing that you can and say, this is my future, or writer, one good phrase that you can build my career upon. Thus, your dream will be anchored in present actions while building a foundation for the future.

Action from right intention, feeling grounded

Action is such a beautiful, simple way to help ourselves to feel better. Buddhist teaching speaks about right action. Right action is acting with positive and helping intent and. helping yourself equally. Helping yourself will automatically benefit those around you when you're connected with your inborn nature of love and compassion. You're not excluding others you by helping yourself first. You are making yourself more highly valuable to them, more comforting, and more considerate. In fact, when you're connected to this essential self of love, there is no separation between helping yourself and helping others. It is the same.

There are times when we can't seemed to help ourselves. This are times when we have no energy, feel a down or tired and don't feel motivated. We may think there's no reason to try to do anything because nothing is going to help anyway. But the smallest right action can begin an immediate change for the better. When you approach tasks with the intention of self-care and self-improvement, opening a window can feel important.

Fear of action

There are times in our life where fear takes charge. We become emotional robots going through the motions of life. It may be a time when emotional pain is crushing, creating depression, phobias, or physical issues. We question our purpose and meaning. Life has no flavor and we don't want to do anything. When 99% of our conscious mind has incapacitated us, rendering us immobile and unable to assist ourselves, it is at this moment that we must depend on the remaining 1% to motivate us into taking action, no matter how small.

When life isn't going your way, act. When you feel discouraged or down, ask yourself to take one step outside your house or apartment. Then stand there and give yourself credit for doing something. Take one full, deep breath. What does that feel like? Keep doing small things for yourself until drop by drop your bucket fills. You don't have to move mountains each and every day. Look for opportunities to do small things for yourself, then do it. Clean the dishes, make the bed. Go to the gym and lift 1 weight or sit in the sauna. Listen to a bird sing. A smile is an action. Smile even if your heart is breaking. Don't expect immediate, earth-shattering changes. Allow the power of action to work for you. You'll feel a little better and a little better more.

Action is energy

Action effectively counters negative energy and self-doubt. During your retreat, you had meaningful experiences and emotions. It is important to understand that these experiences cannot be brought back home; instead, you must create new ones. Maintaining a positive mindset is essential for self-improvement, much like the approach you embraced when you entered treatment. The daily plan helps you continue to act in your highest interests and positive intentions.

The smallest actions can generate energy that promotes further action, positive momentum, and increased resilience. For example, when an individual experiencing depression takes a step outside their home, they may find a slight improvement in their outlook, potentially creating momentum for additional actions. Regardless of how bleak and overwhelming the present moment may appear, choosing inaction and avoidance is itself a form of action. Any action, no matter how minor, can contribute to healing and affirmation; it can counteract negativity, increase energy, and alleviate self-doubt.

How to take action (When you don't feel like it)

Prepare yourself for the ups and downs that life will bring. Make a plan. Many people say when they are feeling down, they engage in specific activities. Find something you enjoy doing and make it your default action. You don't need to convince yourself to enjoy it; just do it without expecting immediate relief from your low mood.

While you are engaged in this activity don't avoid your feelings. Acknowledge that you feel miserable but continue with it anyway. Recognize that although you may not feel entirely okay, there is some part of you that is holding it together. Remind yourself, nobody is perfectly great all the time, if we are honest with ourselves. Life is a roller coaster for everyone. It's riding on the two rails of contentment and satisfaction that is the art of living.

Try something new or revisit an activity you have enjoyed before, regardless of your current state. Don't put any pressure on yourself to talk to anybody or do anything special just do something. Plan and think about these strategies while you are feeling good, knowing that challenges will inevitably come, just like the sun rising and setting each day. Do not anticipate these challenges but be prepared when they inevitably occur.

When you feel overwhelmed, take small steps toward improvement, even if it requires significant effort. The smallest actions can generate momentum that gradually alleviates distress, helping you move forward little by little until you feel better. It takes a lot of courage to do this the first time. But it gets easier and easier. It's a learning and living process.

The Fifth Horseman: Desire, rocket fuel of life.

Desire is the greatest of all life stimulates, acting as rocket fuel for our goals and dreams. When flowing from our true nature, desire is both the greatest motivator and the embodiment of our true-life purpose. This desire is created from the essential self, not the mental yearning for superficial accessories and achievements offered to us by our digital devices. When we are in harmony with a powerful desire force, life becomes vibrant and meaningful. Otherwise, we are wrestling with ourselves. Without desire, life becomes a tasteless exercise occupying space and wasting time.

Without a strong desire, the other horsemen are less likely to be developed, making desire the driving force among the five horsemen. Unless our desire is compelling, when life becomes difficult and challenging, we will lose purpose and give up. Or if you have some extraordinary willpower and fortune, you may achieve your desires only to find they weren't meaningful to you. They are meaningful because you are not connected to your authentic self. All your ideas and wishes stem from a false sense of self built upon the quicksand of popular culture. This leaves us feeling empty and unfulfilled, even while triumphantly standing among the prizes of achievement. These only reward others ideas of success. The difference between superficial and sustained desire lies in those objects of power and achievement enticing us, and the purposeful life we are intended to live.

By tapping into our authentic desire, we navigate our life journey with confidence. Knowing what we want is knowing who we are. We do not lose our way in the turbulence of life. We continue with self-respect and compassion, living our best lives. We will not self-destruct. No more aimlessly searching for a mystical meaning to life. Meaning and desire are linked. Every moment of life becomes meaningful. Profound desire belongs only to us, it is ours and ours alone. It is our truth and value. It's not an obligation we feel to achieve or an attempt to feel worthy. It is the essence of us that needs no explanation or justification. With desire as our beacon, we are on the path of pleasure and the journey becomes as enjoyable as the destination.

Your desire brought you to retreat/treatment.

You were strongly motivated by desire when you came to R/T. Every action you took was propelled by desire. Clearly, you wanted to change your life. You desired to help yourself be better. Your desire may have been *not* to do something or to get *away* from something. You may have been in the middle of a work or relationship problem that you desired personal space and objectivity. You may have had a desire to detox, or to abstain and clean yourself. You may have sought relief from stressful disorders such as anxiety, trauma, or depression. There may have been thoughts you wanted to resolve and find peace with. Whatever it was, your motivation was clear and well defined because you wanted something good for yourself. You had hope and desire of improving your life. This powered you through all the obstacles in your way and the growth you made in R/T. Now, let's keep this working for you as you're returning home.

Connecting to powerful desire.

How do we connect to our true self desire and the power of it? Buddhist teachers say we have a natural desire within us to express our authentic selves, but it is buried beneath a lifetime of conditioning and false ideas. No matter what has happen in our life or how far we have removed ourselves it remains within us. Do we really want that job, spouse, car, or award? If those are in agreement with our purpose, we are satisfied. If not, we feel empty and look to fill our life with diversions or habits. Yet, we need meaning beyond the superficial. that 'meaning' varies with everyone. But the core of it is the same for everyone: self-love and compassion. Some have a deep yearning for family, others for the arts or crafts, and others to teach, heal, and so on. Those could all be good if they're in harmony with our true self. Alignment with our desire and the deep self is e only value measurement of desire is what it means to us personally. If we lose touch with our true nature, we won't see what's inside us. Yet, as the teaching goes, it is within us just the same.

There are methods to reconnect and find the deep self. Our original shining self never vanished. It's within us. Always has been. Through mindful exercises and activities in the daily plan, we can clean our programming and restore ourselves. Cleaning the bugs and malware from our conditioned mind and body connects the whole of us and those desires most inspiring.

Let's not repeat the refrains of childhood; that we are not worthy or capable, we will not be appreciated, or happiness is undeserved. None of that is true. But it is true that these ideas were inserted in our early programming. No matter, by accessing our true self through a process of living consciously, simply called mindfulness, we can connect to this self where strongest desires springs. The old refrains will be forgotten.

Stop saying no to your desires.

Why do you not do what you want most for yourself? We do everything we want without thinking yet deny ourselves those genuine and compelling. Let's stop dismissing emotional desires and give them the value and respect they deserve. Let's look at all of our desires so that we can separate our deep desires and stop chasing shallow, and demoralizing appetites? We allow fear and something called practicality to interfere with the excitement of honest deep desire. In our conditioned minds, we don't deserve or have the right to enjoy ourselves, to follow our greatest dreams. Neglecting our true desires punishes us with a life of frustration. Stop dismission emotional desire as frivolous or meaningless. Honor your emotions. Respect your desires.

Make no apologies or explanations. You have to see everything about yourself before you can make choices. I like people. I like talking or performing in front of people. I like being around animals. I like thinking about ideas or complex problems. When you pay attention to what motivates you, don't dismiss it, respect it. You can't tell yourself, ah, it's not practical or realistic. Practicality will keep you in the dark, wearing the mask of someone you're not happy to see in the mirror. Trust yourself. Give passion a vote in your decision. Expect your desire to change, modify, and transform on your journey. Don't worry if the target moves. What we want now is rarely the same as what we want later. It's not about the target; it's following the path lined with the golden bricks of desire. Following this path is saying yes to yourself.

Let your true desire guide you.

Our emotional desire guides us more faithfully and powerfully than our rational thinking. Use this power and stop dismissing desire as unpractical, unrealistic, or selfish. Let's follow it, see where it leads us, and let it fuel our best self. To make effective and stable decisions, it is essential to first establish a connection with our innermost self. Without this alignment, our choices will lack strength and commitment. Make deliberate decisions to steer away from deceptive gratifications and guide us towards a meaningful and enduring purpose.

When your desire is a true expression of yourself, your purpose and desire are one in harmony. Confusion and conflict diminish. Then, whatever you do will be from human nature's core, self-love, not from fear or self-loathing. No matter what your future goals, each step you take on the journey will be fulfilling because you are walking in harmony with your true self. Deep desire flowing from ones true purpose is a satisfying sensation that cannot be created with thinking. It must be experienced with the quiet, non-thinking self. The daily plan supports this; creating experiences which unite deep desire with true purpose.

3

Daily Program for Best Two Weeks of Your Life

This is a unique, concentrated program which delivers core transformation. Unlike traditional self-help programs which are designed to challenge thoughts and CHANGE beliefs and attitudes through understanding, this program promotes change through NON-THINKING allowing discovery of the true, unburdened self through experience. It is less rational than it is spiritual, more self-accepting than self-regulating. It focuses on creating unique daily experiences, quiet moments of un-think which result in a kind of deeper self-knowledge by the process of subtraction.

Living consciously, or mindfully, is the essence of this program. The activities are not directed towards playing the chess game of life, moving pieces according to habitual strategies OR USING past experiences to project future moves. They're directed towards your best and authentic self. Then all of your moves in the game of life become genuine and satisfying. We can certainly improve our game by thinking a little better, but for fundamental transformation and living a life liberated from empty pursuits, shifting away from the constant chatter of the thinking mind is key. The program cultivates this inner stillness and insightful self-awareness. It nurtures contentment through meditation, mindfulness, and reflection. These proven techniques quiet the mental noise which interferes with one's higher consciousness and joy.

By creating unique experiences and quiet moments of reflection, one gains knowledge of the deep self. It's like having a new, powerful telescope to explore an inner world never before revealed. profound insights and data. The daily program integrates experiential, reflective, and cognitive activities with esteem-building exercises and the development of new sustainable habits.

The primary objective is to practice strategies for maintaining contentment and satisfaction when life's roller coaster swings wildly.

The Activities

The activities in the daily plan are the heart and soul of the best two weeks of your life. If you overlook the rest of the program, this section is self-contained, offering practical, step-by-step personal activities that can resolve an unhappy and unrewarding life. These will impact you more deeply than you've ever experienced. These will teach you to maintain calm and peace within the chaos of life. Doing these will engage your original, authentic self where lies your meaning and purpose. All of this and more will flow from practicing and using the daily program.

These activities seem simple, too simple to be so powerful, but simplicity is precisely their power. they appear simple because no thinking is required. To stop thinking is the first objective. What's our reality when we quiet the noise within the mind? Who are we really when we create space from our thoughts? Let's drop into our deeper, higher self where ideas are not blocking authenticity. Until one does this, there cannot be transformation or liberation of one's life. When we rely on thought and let it control us, it prevents us from revealing our best self. Life becomes easier and rewarding when we use our limited time in this profound state of being authentic.

We are not supposes to think? Of course, we think. We need our minds, but we need to be the master of our minds and not have our minds mastering us by jumping from one thought to the next. I can be thinking and be aware of my sensations in my body. I can walk knowing I'm pressing my feet on the earth and hearing the wind and the birds all around me. My thoughts come and go without me attaching to them. In this way I am free. I haven't stopped thinking, but I'm in the moment living my life. I see my thoughts but they don't entice me. When I want to think and play interesting life games, I do so with more clarity and judgment. I am able to live my life with sensation and passion. I create balance between thoughts and non-thinking, and space from thought with silence.

Be patient with yourself as you engage in this self-exploration. Maintain your effort for two weeks and you will see and feel benefits. The path to transformation is not always straightforward, expect to be surprised. To experience the profound insights which arise from deeper states of consciousness requires courage, an open mind, and, above all, total self-acceptance. In this way you will uncover an authentic sense of being that transcends the limitations imposed by the thinking mind. If thinking a little better could create a life with richness of sensation nourishing every day then this would be taught in schools and universities. The way is by engaging ourselves without the distractions and burden of our constant thoughts.

Focus is the tool used for this and the capacity to focus is strengthened while doing these practices. Focus, the first horseman, creates space between our monkey mind and our quiet self. The method to increase focus is to choose an object and maintain focus upon that object. We want to add strength to focus even in the middle of an emotional hurricane. So simple to say yet challenging to do until we develop focus and concentration. Nearly every activity in the program has a focusing procedure. When your mind wanders or becomes distracted from the object, you simply bring your focus back to the object. Practicing in this way creates a stream of benefits.

Each of the daily procedures has a recording in the link provided which will guide you. Listen to the recordings until you can do them from memory or any time you want to refresh the procedures. You can read the procedures for further explanation or for understanding the goal of each activity.

It's important to do the procedures as designed. Though simple, they are specific, created to have an immediate and long-lasting impact upon your well-being. By enhancing concentration skills, they establish a tranquil space between your overwhelming thoughts and your calm, serene self. Don't expect anything, observe everything, and don't strive for results. Let the process give you what you need. By consistently engaging in the activities and procedures each day, you will begin to clearly see the benefits.

The Worksheets

The reflective worksheets help you to see life more clearly by bringing your thoughts out of your dark head, onto paper (computer), and into the light. They connect your emotional desires to your intellectual choices. By observing yourself more clearly, you understand yourself and the forces pressuring you. You'll see more options for acting truthfully to yourself. Are wasteful habits directing your happiness and well-being, overriding your desires? Let's look at the reality instead of believing our deceptive self-delusions.

Stand back and take a look. I like to think of these work-growth sheets like little white birds circling overhead looking down and seeing the shape of our lives as they truly are. Not our delusions of life rumbling around in our heads, but the life we're in fact constructing. Our truth. Before we can transform ourselves into our best version of self, we need to see clearly. This process eliminates the illusions we uphold, enabling us to address our objective reality. Seeing reality is crucial for improving our lives. Be your white bird above, honestly observing yourself by using these work-growth sheets.

DAILY 1 PLAN FOCUS SELF
Spending time, Wasting time

DAILY 1 PLAN
FOCUS ON SELF

	Minutes	✓

Morning

	Minutes	
Big Breathing with bell (R)	20	○
Gate Gate Chanting (R)	5	○

Day

Mindful Walking (R)	5	○
Stress Reduction Count Breathing	As Needed	○
Instruction - How to's reading	10	○

Lunch - Mindful Eating (R) ○

Evening

Big Breathing 3 X Before Dinner	11	○

Dinner - Eating Mindfully (R) ○

~Work Sheets~

Day 1 Plan	8	○
Spending-Wasting Time	5	○
My Good Day	2	○
Vow for Tomorrow	4	○

Bedtime

Relaxation and Confidence Procedure (R)	20	○

Total Time For Myself Today   /80   Total Circles Checked   _____

DOWNLOAD AUDIO instructions/Meditations from free link: https://bit.ly/4iG4wQj

Instructions step by step for the Daily Plan

Read the procedures here or follow the link and download the daily recordings. Use the recordings. some you will memorize. The big breathing procedures can be used with or without recordings after you have them memorized.

Big Breathing with Bell Procedure

1. begin by breathing in through your nose to the count of 10
2. 2, count silently to yourself
3. When you reach 10 let go of your breath
4. Repeat breathing and counting 10 times, On the 6th breath hold your breath counting to 20 before releasing.

This procedure is for mental clarity and calm. It uses two very important techniques. One is counting your breath, an ancient Buddhist technique for concentrating your mind. be sure to count silently to yourself.

The second technique is expanding your breathing instrument by breathing into a relaxed stomach then, when that fills, fill your chest until it rises, then, ultimately, your diaphragm stretches. this is stretching from the inside out. this techniques releases chronic tension in your breathing instrument which was created by childhood trauma and continues to reinforce repression and avoidance with every breath.

Gate gate power chanting 5 minutes

1. Gate Gate Para Gate Para Sam Gate Bodhi Swaha. Say the words from the heart sutra in rhythm with the wood drum
2. focus you mind on the sound coming out of your mouth and on the vibration of the sound falling deep within your body.
3. When you mind wanders come back to the sound.
4. Chanting is a method of being in the moment that even practitioners with little concentration skill find easy and beneficial. The object to focus

upon as the sound while being aware of the vibration of the sound deep within your body. It's great for learning to focus. One feels an opening of life channels and can be experienced as a tingling throughout the body or Lightheadedness from clearing the mind. When it is difficult to focus the mind sitting quietly this chanting in the Zen style Is like a laser cleaning thoughts.

Mindfully walking with counting breath

- Stand relaxed and feel the earth beneath your feet.

1. Take a deep breath and feel the pressure of your feet upon the earth.
2. Begin by walking with our left foot and inhaling to the count of four and exhaling to the count of four while focusing with our mind's eye on the bottom of our feet.
3. Counting silently to yourself relax your shoulders and let your arms swing lightly and easily.
4. Notice your weight shifting from right to left and heel to toe

Mindfully walking procedures. Walk with the peace of monks. Walk to clear your mind and relax. Put your focus on the bottom of your feet and upon your breath. When your mind wanders or distracted, come back to the counting or the pressure of your foot on the earth. whenever you want to be free of your monkey mind you can stop counting and walk quietly with no thinking and no judging. Walk focusing on your sensations of being here now. Walk mindfully WHEREVER you go.

Stress reduction count breathing

1. Begin breathing in through your nose and out through your mouth all of the air that you can possibly inhale and exhale
2. Relax all the tension in your body; in your shoulders and neck, your tongue and your throat.
3. Round your stomach forward to make room for your diaphragm and begin breathing deeply into your stomach.
4. Count your breath 6 inhale through your nose and six out through your mouth.

5. If your mind wanders to your thoughts or feelings, come back to the count and focus upon counting your breath.
6. Repeat 30 times.

We're using the ancient Buddhist technique of counting your breath to create space between you're busy, spinning 40,000 daily thoughts, and your quiet peaceful self. With each breath you become more relaxed and it will become easier to focus up on your breath. We don't stop thinking; we focus away from it. The more often you do this the stronger your focus will become. Strength of focus is gives us peace from our monkey minds, and allows us to maintain this calm during the ups and downs of life.

Instruction. How to's reading.

1. Look in the index of the how to's, section 5 And choose any topic that you're curious about. There's no benefit to be reading these in order.
2. Read as much or as little as you wish. Your only obligation is to please yourself.

Big breathing 3x power

1. three sets of 6 big breaths, holding to 20

This is a slightly longer version of big breathing. you will hold your sixth breath three times instead of once. This holding a full breath will give you a nice internal stretch of your breathing instrument freeing yourself from physical-emotional tension. counting to 6 only, not ten, three times. Particularly good when you're more agitated and stressed and need more calm immediately.

Mindfully Eating

1. look at your food Or drink. Observe the shape of the plate or vessel. Notice the colors, size, and form. Observe it's temperature and texture. See all the details that you can.
2. Pick up the utensil or cup slash glass. Feel its temperature in your fingertips. Notice the weight in your hand and arm.
3. Take a bite or a drink. Put down and release the cup/glass or the utensil Notice the sensations from your lips to your tongue. Observe the texture

in your mouth.
4. chew or drink slowly, at least three times longer than you normally do before you swallow. Notice how the food mingles with your mouth and changes it's character.
5. Swallow and notice the food falling into your body. You may observe a sensation beginning in your stomach and moving through your body. Smile and observe that.

When we focus upon what we're doing we're doing things mindfully. We focus upon the sensory stimulation of holding a fork, seen the colors and texture of food, And so on. We focus upon our perceptions, This heightens our AWARENESS AND gives us space from our busy mind. Notice that you eat less the more you practice this and that food tastes better and is more satisfying.

Relaxation and confidence breathing procedure

1. lie down in a comfortable place. You may use headphones or earbuds, and cover your eyes if you wish.
2. There's nothing to do but relax and listen.

This is a passive relaxation method. Tension is the life killer and this simple relaxation procedure has the power to change lives By releasing deep seated tension. Anytime you need to recharge, feel worn down, or want to sleep more deeply listen to the recording. It's OK to fall asleep. accept whatever your response. It will be working for you subconsciously. You can listen to it several times a day if you wish. You will begin functioning at a higher level almost immediately.

Gratitude energy meditation

1. listen lying down or sitting relaxed and undisturbed.
2. Don't think about the words but let them wash through you, trusting your intuitive self to connect with the ideas.

This meditation plants seeds of positivity and encouragement. It promotes profound relaxation releasing TENSION from negativity and pain. It combines positive affirmations with one's true nature of love and compassion.

Gate gate 15

1. This is the same procedure as power chanting 5 but little longer.
2. It gives you more time to relax and to align your breathing with the chant.

Maintaining focus for longer periods drops us deeper into our true nature, our original self. Some days you may want to do this Twice for a more transcendent experience. It is a wonderful method for walking through the gate of liberation and aspiring to a higher consciousness.

Four position tongue release

1. Position 1, stick your tongue out as far as it will go and breathe in deeply One breath.
2. Permit your face, your forehead and your neck to let go of your tongue.
3. Position 2, place the tip of your tongue lightly behind your lower lip and repeat the process of 1 deep breath.
4. Position 3, bring your tongue in lightly behind your lower teeth, allowing your jaw to relax. It may require more release of your facial muscles. Take one very deep breath.
5. Position 4, allow your tongue to rise into your mouth to a position where there is absolutely no tension. Wherever it goes this is the neutral position free from emotional agitation. Take one very deep breath.

So this is one of the outside in relaxation procedures. In the same way one gets a massage, stretches, or does yoga this relaxes the tongue. It brings focus to and release our tongue and our throat and everything else along the vagus nerve corridor. This this major nerve sends agitating signals from our belly to our minds. This procedure relaxes this quarter and frees one from much of this agitation. All tension is connected and you will notice your entire body relaxing as you do this procedure.

1. COMFORTING VIBRATION PROCEDURE
2. Inhale through your nose while counting silently to six.

3. When you have filled your stomach, chest, and your diaphragm expands, say the word Mu until the breath is too weak for sound.
4. Repeat this five times.
5. Follow the same procedure but now say the word vu.
6. Repeat this four times
7. follow the same procedure but now say the word ah
8. repeat this three times.
9. When finished, Ask yourself two questions; Which word created the most intense sensation vibration, and where in your body was the center of each one of those word vibrations?

Do this procedure to comfort yourself. If there's an intense emotion, a bit overwhelming, follow this procedure for calm. You may want to do this at night before you go to sleep and have a more comforting peaceful sleep. We use humming and vibrations naturally to comfort ourselves. The more often you practice this, the greater effect it will have.

DAILY 1 REVIEW
Spending time, Wasting time

DAILY 1 REVIEW
SPENDING OR WASTING TIME

How I Spent My Time Today	Date __/__/____	Time Wasted	Time Spent Well
	Sleep		
	Paid Work		
	Eating - Cooking		
	Personal Grooming		
	Healthcare - Exercise - Sport		
	Shopping - Errand - House Care		
	Travel - Driving		
	School - Education		
	Group Friends - Social		
	Individual Friends		
	Family - Children - Partner		
	Wellness - Yoga / Zen - Spiritual		
	Personal Practices - Mindful / Read - Think - Hobby		
	Social - Computer - Media - Games - Communication		
	Entertainment - Movies - Theater - Live Music		
	Caring for Others - Charity		
	Quiet or Alone		
	Total		

Instructions for Spending Time Wasting Time

"We're either spending time or wasting time, and once gone, it's gone forever," Bruce Lee, actor and martial art master.

Taking a few moments to see how you actually spend your time may surprise you. What are we doing? Time-use data is vital to show us how much of our life we're spending our wasting. Once we see how we're living, we can better choose our time spent. Are we living according to our true purpose in life. What choices are we making that waste precious time with meaningless and hollow activities? Those things that you enjoyed and want to repeat reflect your deeper desire. They will have staying power and move you forward one step at a time. You will be excited about them. Could we live differently? You can start planning your days to give you more time doing what you desire.

Let's track each day by counting time as carefully as we count money. Time is more valuable. Let's look at our life as it actually is without fooling or misleading ourselves. No judgments or criticisms, just be accurate. It's not easy to look at ourselves but until we see our life honestly, we wander. Time doesn't lie, but we will lie to ourselves until the bitter end. Knowing is power to change.

Put the amount of time in either the spending or wasting shape next to the activity. Sleeping is thought up as a good and necessary way to spend your time, not waste it. But if you don't prepare yourself for a good night's sleep by eating or drinking late before you go to bed or distracting your sleep with television or social media running in the background, you could be wasting your opportunity for sleep and self-limiting energy for tomorrow. In this way, a portion of sleep time can be listed as wasting time.

Similarly with eating. Eating healthy and reasonable quantities nourishes you, giving you strength and vigor to live your best life. This is spending time well eating. But if you're eating to calm your anxiety or to avoid or dull your feelings then you're wasting your time. In this way, eating could be both wasted and spent during the day and have both circle and square with time.

Paid work is another activity which may have both beneficial spent and wasted in it. Think of this activity as an adventure looking for gold in your life. The answer to the question, what am I doing that I really enjoy, and I want to do more of, is the golden treasure ..

Doing this 'Spending time, Wasting Time' worksheet takes courage to see yourself but this activity will build self-esteem. This is not about accusing YOURSELF; it's honoring and respecting yourself. Add up the hours(0.1 hour equals 6 minutes) at the bottom of the page to get a general idea of what your life direction is. Circle the activities you did during the day that were most exciting or satisfying and that you want to do more of tomorrow. this will give you direction for deeper satisfaction and contentment. Square those activities you feel you wasted your time and that you wish to minimize tomorrow.

Nobody will score this but you. Your life is the test, and you are the teacher and the student. This process is to see it, think about it, then take a step towards it. You actually become more of who you want to be. You become more the authentic you. Discover the you who is excited about life.

You'll notice yourself wasting time on activities which offer only a temporary payoff. They do not energize you and create forward movement. The superficial wants of fame, possessions, and money do not provide motivation in difficult times. Try to target those activities which flow from your true nature. Activities based upon this deeper desire will give satisfaction and contentment.

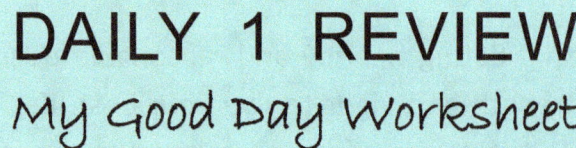

DAILY 1 REVIEW
My Good Day Worksheet

DAILY 1 PLAN
MY GOOD DAY

TODAY I MOST ENJOYED DOING...

TODAY I MOST ENJOYED SEEING/WATCHING...

TODAY I ENJOYED MYSELF WHEN...

TODAY I WAS AMAZED /PLEASED WHEN I RECEIVED THIS HELP/SUPPORT...

APPLAUSE TO ME

ONE THING I DID TODAY I GIVE MYSELF APPLAUSE IS...

10. Instructions for My Good Day Worksheet

This work-growth sheet may be the simplest yet most difficult to do. It's simply asking yourself what you enjoy. Many people feel unworthy to really enjoy themselves, to receive nourishment from their lives. They're always striving for something more never pausing to give themselves credit or complement. They feel guilty if they stop. They were brought up to think they were only worthwhile if they were striving for more. Because no one in their family was satisfied with them, they are never satisfied with themselves. They have to prove themselves to somebody, somewhere, without end. Enjoyment is not the point.

The answers you write need to come from your belly not your mind. From what activity brought a smile or sense of satisfaction to you. Separate the feeling of obligation from the pleasure of doing. It's not about what you did to survive, but what you did to thrive. There may be nothing that you connected in this day so don't force it. Be true to yourself by not faking it.

Set your mind to look for enjoyment tomorrow. When you start evaluating your activities for excitement and deep pleasure you'll start finding them. Temporary and superficial desires will not fuel you past the depressions and distractions of life. We want and deserve to live a juicy life. you have the right to be happy, you don't have to earn it. We want to have reasons to get up in the morning, clap our hands together and say, this is going to be a great day. If this is too much to ask of ourselves, then what is our life's purpose? ,

DAILY 1 REVIEW
Vows for Tomorrow worksheet

DAILY 1 REVIEW
VOWS FOR TOMORROW

01. For Enjoying Myself

I vow to spend 5 minutes more tomorrow enjoying…

_____

02. For Growing my knowledge

I vow to spend 5 minutes more tomorrow reading or listening…

_____

03. For Improving my Health

I vow to spend 5 minutes more tomorrow breaking one habit food or smoking or eating…

_____

04. For My compassion to others

I vow to spend 5 minutes more to praise or boost two friends …

_____

Instructions for Vow for Tomorrow worksheet

Making a daily vow to yourself is a concrete, self-affirming action. This process is self-affirming. Composing a mental goal with your emotional commitment to take action. By making this vow you're saying, I want this, it is important to me. With the bricks of personal passion, you're building a road in the direction you want to go.

These vows will give you clear direction instead of wandering lost in flashy ideas and common views. Without vows, or promises to yourself, as the road becomes difficult, you will lose your way. When the old self-defeating habits grind down your best intentions, the vows you make will give you strength to continue.

These simple vow worksheets are very powerful. Your vow reflects your life philosophy, values, and the better person you aspire to be. It's vowing from the true you, without self-censorship or judgment. These vows are for taking immediate action the next day, yet they are steps towards a longer self-commitment. Making a vow and taking immediate steps, no matter how small, creates strong momentum for living your best life. And the vows made in the night grows your intuitive and creative powers for tomorrow.

DAILY Program
Days 2 Through 14

DAILY 2 PLAN
FOCUS ON SELF

	Minutes	✓

Morning
- Big Breathing with bell (R) — 20 — ○
- Gate Gate Chanting (R) — 5 — ○

Day
- Mindful Walking (R) — 5 — ○
- Stress Reduction Count Breathing — As Needed — ○
- Instruction – How to's reading — 10 — ○

Lunch – Mindful Eating (R) ○

Evening
- Big Breathing 3 X Before Dinner — 11 — ○

Dinner – Eating Mindfully (R) ○

~Work Sheets~
- Day 2 Plan — 8 — ○
- Spending-Wasting Time — 5 — ○
- My Good Day — 2 — ○
- Vow for Tomorrow — 4 — ○

Bedtime
- Relaxation and Confidence Procedure (R) — 20 — ○

Total Time For Myself Today   /80   Total Circles Checked   _____

DAILY 2 REVIEW
SPENDING OR WASTING TIME

How I Spent My Time Today Date __/__/____	Time Wasted	Time Spent Well
Sleep		
Paid Work		
Eating - Cooking		
Personal Grooming		
Healthcare - Exercise - Sport		
Shopping - Errand - House Care		
Travel - Driving		
School - Education		
Group Friends - Social		
Individual Friends		
Family - Children - Partner		
Wellness - Yoga / Zen - Spiritual		
Personal Practices - Mindful / Read - Think - Hobby		
Social - Computer - Media - Games - Communication		
Entertainment - Movies - Theater - Live Music		
Caring for Others - Charity		
Quiet or Alone		
Total		

DAILY 2 PLAN
MY GOOD DAY

TODAY I MOST ENJOYED DOING...

TODAY I MOST ENJOYED SEEING/WATCHING...

TODAY I ENJOYED MYSELF WHEN...

TODAY I WAS AMAZED /PLEASED WHEN I RECEIVED THIS HELP/SUPPORT...

APPLAUSE TO ME

ONE THING I DID TODAY I GIVE MYSELF APPLAUSE IS...

DAILY 2 REVIEW
VOWS FOR TOMORROW

01. For Enjoying Myself

I vow to spend 5 minutes more tomorrow enjoying...

_____

02. For Growing my knowledge

I vow to spend 5 minutes more tomorrow reading or listening...

_____

03. For Improving my Health

I vow to spend 5 minutes more tomorrow breaking one habit food or smoking or eating...

_____

04. For My compassion to others

I vow to spend 5 minutes more to praise or boost two friends ...

_____

DAILY 3 PLAN
FOCUS ON SELF

	Minutes	✓

Morning

Big Breathing with bell (R)	20	○
Gate Gate Chanting (R)	5	○

Day

Mindful Walking (R)	5	○
Stress Reduction Count Breathing	As Needed	○
Instruction – How to's reading	10	○

Lunch – Mindful Eating (R) ○

Evening

Big Breathing 3 X Before Dinner	11	○

Dinner – Eating Mindfully (R) ○

~Work Sheets~

Day 3 Plan	8	○
Spending-Wasting Time	5	○
My Good Day	2	○
Vow for Tomorrow	4	○

Bedtime

Relaxation and Confidence Procedure (R)	20	○

Total Time For Myself Today   /80   Total Circles Checked   _____

DAILY 3 REVIEW
SPENDING OR WASTING TIME

How I Spent My Time Today Date __/__/____	Time Wasted	Time Spent Well
Sleep		
Paid Work		
Eating - Cooking		
Personal Grooming		
Healthcare - Exercise - Sport		
Shopping - Errand - House Care		
Travel - Driving		
School - Education		
Group Friends - Social		
Individual Friends		
Family - Children - Partner		
Wellness - Yoga / Zen - Spiritual		
Personal Practices - Mindful / Read - Think - Hobby		
Social - Computer - Media - Games - Communication		
Entertainment - Movies - Theater - Live Music		
Caring for Others - Charity		
Quiet or Alone		
Total		

DAILY 3 PLAN
MY GOOD DAY

TODAY I MOST ENJOYED DOING...

TODAY I MOST ENJOYED SEEING/WATCHING...

TODAY I ENJOYED MYSELF WHEN...

TODAY I WAS AMAZED /PLEASED WHEN I RECEIVED THIS HELP/SUPPORT...

APPLAUSE TO ME

ONE THING I DID TODAY I GIVE MYSELF APPLAUSE IS...

DAILY 3 REVIEW
VOWS FOR TOMORROW

01. For Enjoying Myself

I vow to spend 5 minutes more tomorrow enjoying...

_____

02. For Growing my knowledge

I vow to spend 5 minutes more tomorrow reading or listening...

_____

03. For Improving my Health

I vow to spend 5 minutes more tomorrow breaking one habit food or smoking or eating...

_____

04. For My compassion to others

I vow to spend 5 minutes more to praise or boost two friends ...

_____

DAILY 4 PLAN
FOCUS ON SELF

	Minutes	✓

Morning
- Big Breathing with bell (R) — 20 — ○
- Gate Gate Chanting (R) — 5 — ○

Day
- Mindful Walking (R) — 5 — ○
- Stress Reduction Count Breathing — As Needed — ○
- Instruction - How to's reading — 10 — ○

Lunch - Mindful Eating (R) ○

Evening
- Big Breathing 3 X Before Dinner — 11 — ○

Dinner - Eating Mindfully (R) ○

~Work Sheets~
- Day 4 Plan — 8 — ○
- Spending-Wasting Time — 5 — ○
- My Good Day — 2 — ○
- Vow for Tomorrow — 4 — ○

Bedtime
- Relaxation and Confidence Procedure (R) — 20 — ○

Total Time For Myself Today   /80   Total Circles Checked   _____

DAILY 4 REVIEW
SPENDING OR WASTING TIME

How I Spent My Time Today Date __/__/____	Time Wasted	Time Spent Well
Sleep		
Paid Work		
Eating - Cooking		
Personal Grooming		
Healthcare - Exercise - Sport		
Shopping - Errand - House Care		
Travel - Driving		
School - Education		
Group Friends - Social		
Individual Friends		
Family - Children - Partner		
Wellness - Yoga / Zen - Spiritual		
Personal Practices - Mindful / Read - Think - Hobby		
Social - Computer - Media - Games - Communication		
Entertainment - Movies - Theater - Live Music		
Caring for Others - Charity		
Quiet or Alone		
Total		

DAILY 4 PLAN
MY GOOD DAY

TODAY I MOST ENJOYED DOING...

TODAY I MOST ENJOYED SEEING/WATCHING...

TODAY I ENJOYED MYSELF WHEN...

TODAY I WAS AMAZED /PLEASED WHEN I RECEIVED THIS HELP/SUPPORT...

APPLAUSE TO ME

ONE THING I DID TODAY I GIVE MYSELF APPLAUSE IS...

DAILY 4 REVIEW
VOWS FOR TOMORROW

01. For Enjoying Myself

I vow to spend 5 minutes more tomorrow enjoying...

_____

02. For Growing my knowledge

I vow to spend 5 minutes more tomorrow reading or listening...

_____

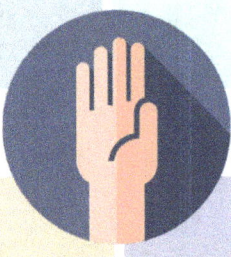

03. For Improving my Health

I vow to spend 5 minutes more tomorrow breaking one habit food or smoking or eating...

_____

04. For My compassion to others

I vow to spend 5 minutes more to praise or boost two friends...

_____

DAILY 5 PLAN
FOCUS ON SELF

	Minutes	✓

Morning
	Minutes	
Big Breathing with bell (R)	20	○
Gate Gate Chanting (R)	5	○

Day
Mindful Walking (R)	5	○
Stress Reduction Count Breathing	As Needed	○
Instruction - How to's reading	10	○

Lunch - Mindful Eating (R) ○

Big Breathing 3 X Before Dinner	11	○

Evening

Dinner - Eating Mindfully (R) ○

~Work Sheets~
Day 5 Plan	8	○
Spending-Wasting Time	5	○
My Good Day	2	○
Vow for Tomorrow	4	○

Bedtime
Relaxation and Confidence Procedure (R)	20	○

Total Time For Myself Today   /80   Total Circles Checked   _____

DAILY 5 REVIEW
SPENDING OR WASTING TIME

How I Spent My Time Today Date __/__/____	Time Wasted	Time Spent Well
Sleep		
Paid Work		
Eating - Cooking		
Personal Grooming		
Healthcare - Exercise - Sport		
Shopping - Errand - House Care		
Travel - Driving		
School - Education		
Group Friends - Social		
Individual Friends		
Family - Children - Partner		
Wellness - Yoga / Zen - Spiritual		
Personal Practices - Mindful / Read - Think - Hobby		
Social - Computer - Media - Games - Communication		
Entertainment - Movies - Theater - Live Music		
Caring for Others - Charity		
Quiet or Alone		
Total		

DAILY 5 PLAN
MY GOOD DAY

TODAY I MOST ENJOYED DOING...

TODAY I MOST ENJOYED SEEING/WATCHING...

TODAY I ENJOYED MYSELF WHEN...

TODAY I WAS AMAZED /PLEASED WHEN I RECEIVED THIS HELP/SUPPORT...

APPLAUSE TO ME

ONE THING I DID TODAY I GIVE MYSELF APPLAUSE IS...

DAILY 5 REVIEW
VOWS FOR TOMORROW

01. For Enjoying Myself

I vow to spend 5 minutes more tomorrow enjoying…

_____

02. For Growing my knowledge

I vow to spend 5 minutes more tomorrow reading or listening…

_____

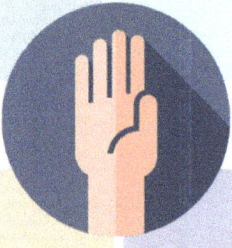

03. For Improving my Health

I vow to spend 5 minutes more tomorrow breaking one habit food or smoking or eating…

_____

04. For My compassion to others

I vow to spend 5 minutes more to praise or boost two friends …

_____

DAILY 6 PLAN
FOCUS ON SELF

	Minutes	✓

Morning
- Big Breathing with bell (R) — 20 — ○
- Gate Gate Chanting (R) — 5 — ○
- Four Position Tongue Release (R) — ○

Day
- Mindful Walking (R) — 5 — ○
- Stress Reduction Count Breathing — As Needed — ○
- Instruction – How to's reading — 10 — ○

Lunch – Mindful Eating (R) ○

Evening
- Big Breathing 3 X Before Dinner — 11 — ○

Dinner – Eating Mindfully (R) ○

~Work Sheets~
- Day 6 Plan — 8 — ○
- Spending-Wasting Time — 5 — ○
- My Good Day — 2 — ○
- Vow for Tomorrow — 4 — ○

Bedtime
- Relaxation and Confidence Procedure (R) — 20 — ○

Total Time For Myself Today   /80   Total Circles Checked   _____

DAILY 6 REVIEW
SPENDING OR WASTING TIME

How I Spent My Time Today Date __/__/____	Time Wasted	Time Spent Well
Sleep		
Paid Work		
Eating - Cooking		
Personal Grooming		
Healthcare - Exercise - Sport		
Shopping - Errand - House Care		
Travel - Driving		
School - Education		
Group Friends - Social		
Individual Friends		
Family - Children - Partner		
Wellness - Yoga / Zen - Spiritual		
Personal Practices - Mindful / Read - Think - Hobby		
Social - Computer - Media - Games - Communication		
Entertainment - Movies - Theater - Live Music		
Caring for Others - Charity		
Quiet or Alone		
Total		

DAILY 6 PLAN
MY GOOD DAY

TODAY I MOST ENJOYED DOING...

TODAY I MOST ENJOYED SEEING/WATCHING...

TODAY I ENJOYED MYSELF WHEN...

TODAY I WAS AMAZED /PLEASED WHEN I RECEIVED THIS HELP/SUPPORT...

APPLAUSE TO ME

ONE THING I DID TODAY I GIVE MYSELF APPLAUSE IS...

DAILY 6 REVIEW
VOWS FOR TOMORROW

01. For Enjoying Myself

I vow to spend 5 minutes more tomorrow enjoying...

_____

02. For Growing my knowledge

I vow to spend 5 minutes more tomorrow reading or listening...

_____

03. For Improving my Health

I vow to spend 5 minutes more tomorrow breaking one habit food or smoking or eating...

_____

04. For My compassion to others

I vow to spend 5 minutes more to praise or boost two friends ...

_____

DAILY 7 PLAN
FOCUS ON SELF

	Minutes	✓

Morning
	Minutes	
Big Breathing with bell (R)	20	○
Gate Gate Chanting (R)	5	○
Four Position Tongue Release (R)		○

Day
	Minutes	
Mindful Walking (R)	5	○
Stress Reduction Count Breathing	As Needed	○
Instruction - How to's reading	10	○

Lunch - Mindful Eating (R) ○

Evening
	Minutes	
Big Breathing 3 X Before Dinner	11	○

Dinner - Eating Mindfully (R) ○

~Work Sheets~
	Minutes	
Day 7 Plan	8	○
Spending-Wasting Time	5	○
My Good Day	2	○
Vow for Tomorrow	4	○

Bedtime
	Minutes	
Relaxation and Confidence Procedure (R)	20	○

Total Time For Myself Today   /80   Total Circles Checked   _____

DAILY 7 REVIEW
SPENDING OR WASTING TIME

How I Spent My Time Today Date __/__/____	Time Wasted	Time Spent Well
Sleep		
Paid Work		
Eating - Cooking		
Personal Grooming		
Healthcare - Exercise - Sport		
Shopping - Errand - House Care		
Travel - Driving		
School - Education		
Group Friends - Social		
Individual Friends		
Family - Children - Partner		
Wellness - Yoga / Zen - Spiritual		
Personal Practices - Mindful / Read - Think - Hobby		
Social - Computer - Media - Games - Communication		
Entertainment - Movies - Theater - Live Music		
Caring for Others - Charity		
Quiet or Alone		
Total		

DAILY 7 PLAN
MY GOOD DAY

TODAY I MOST ENJOYED DOING...

TODAY I MOST ENJOYED SEEING/WATCHING...

TODAY I ENJOYED MYSELF WHEN...

TODAY I WAS AMAZED /PLEASED WHEN I RECEIVED THIS HELP/SUPPORT...

APPLAUSE TO ME

ONE THING I DID TODAY I GIVE MYSELF APPLAUSE IS...

DAILY 7 REVIEW
VOWS FOR TOMORROW

01. **For Enjoying Myself**

I vow to spend 5 minutes more tomorrow enjoying…

_____

02. **For Growing my knowledge**

I vow to spend 5 minutes more tomorrow reading or listening…

_____

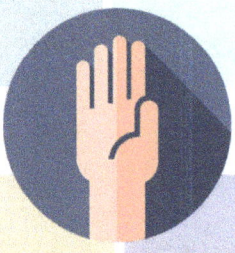

03. **For Improving my Health**

I vow to spend 5 minutes more tomorrow breaking one habit food or smoking or eating…

_____

04. **For My compassion to others**

I vow to spend 5 minutes more to praise or boost two friends …

_____

DAILY 8 PLAN
FOCUS ON SELF

	Minutes	✓

Morning
- Big Breathing with bell (R) — 20 ○
- Gate Gate Chanting (R) — 5 ○
- Four Position Tongue Release (R) — 1 ○

Day
- Mindful Walking (R) — 5 ○
- Stress Reduction Count Breathing — As Needed ○
- Instruction – How to's reading — 10 ○

Lunch – Mindful Eating (R) ○

Evening
- Big Breathing 3 X Before Dinner — 11 ○

Dinner – Eating Mindfully (R) ○

~Work Sheets~
- Day 8 Plan — 8 ○
- Spending-Wasting Time — 5 ○
- My Good Day — 2 ○
- Vow for Tomorrow — 4 ○

Bedtime
- Relaxation and Confidence Procedure (R) — 20 ○

Total Time For Myself Today   /80   Total Circles Checked   _____

DAILY 8 REVIEW
SPENDING OR WASTING TIME

How I Spent My Time Today	Date __/__/____	Time Wasted	Time Spent Well
	Sleep		
	Paid Work		
	Eating - Cooking		
	Personal Grooming		
	Healthcare - Exercise - Sport		
	Shopping - Errand - House Care		
	Travel - Driving		
	School - Education		
	Group Friends - Social		
	Individual Friends		
	Family - Children - Partner		
	Wellness - Yoga / Zen - Spiritual		
	Personal Practices - Mindful / Read - Think - Hobby		
	Social - Computer - Media - Games - Communication		
	Entertainment - Movies - Theater - Live Music		
	Caring for Others - Charity		
	Quiet or Alone		
	Total		

DAILY 8 PLAN
MY GOOD DAY

TODAY I MOST ENJOYED DOING...

TODAY I MOST ENJOYED SEEING/WATCHING...

TODAY I ENJOYED MYSELF WHEN...

TODAY I WAS AMAZED /PLEASED WHEN I RECEIVED THIS HELP/SUPPORT...

APPLAUSE TO ME

ONE THING I DID TODAY I GIVE MYSELF APPLAUSE IS...

DAILY 8 REVIEW
VOWS FOR TOMORROW

01. **For Enjoying Myself**

I vow to spend 5 minutes more tomorrow enjoying...

_____

02. **For Growing my knowledge**

I vow to spend 5 minutes more tomorrow reading or listening...

_____

03. **For Improving my Health**

I vow to spend 5 minutes more tomorrow breaking one habit food or smoking or eating...

_____

04. **For My compassion to others**

I vow to spend 5 minutes more to praise or boost two friends ...

_____

DAILY 9 PLAN
FOCUS ON SELF

	Minutes	✓

Morning
- Big Breathing with bell (R) — 20 ○
- Gate Gate Chanting (R) — 5 ○
- Four Position Tongue Release (R) — 1 ○

Day
- Mindful Walking (R) — 5 ○
- Stress Reduction Count Breathing — As Needed ○
- Instruction - How to's reading — 10 ○

Lunch - Mindful Eating (R) ○

Evening
- Big Breathing 3 X Before Dinner — 11 ○

Dinner - Eating Mindfully (R) ○

~Work Sheets~
- Day 9 Plan — 8 ○
- Spending-Wasting Time — 5 ○
- My Good Day — 2 ○
- Vow for Tomorrow — 4 ○

Bedtime
- Relaxation and Confidence Procedure (R) — 20 ○

Total Time For Myself Today   /80   Total Circles Checked   _____

DAILY 9 REVIEW
SPENDING OR WASTING TIME

How I Spent My Time Today Date __/__/____	Time Wasted	Time Spent Well
Sleep		
Paid Work		
Eating - Cooking		
Personal Grooming		
Healthcare - Exercise - Sport		
Shopping - Errand - House Care		
Travel - Driving		
School - Education		
Group Friends - Social		
Individual Friends		
Family - Children - Partner		
Wellness - Yoga / Zen - Spiritual		
Personal Practices - Mindful / Read - Think - Hobby		
Social - Computer - Media - Games - Communication		
Entertainment - Movies - Theater - Live Music		
Caring for Others - Charity		
Quiet or Alone		
Total		

DAILY 9 PLAN
MY GOOD DAY

TODAY I MOST ENJOYED DOING...

TODAY I MOST ENJOYED SEEING/WATCHING...

TODAY I ENJOYED MYSELF WHEN...

TODAY I WAS AMAZED /PLEASED WHEN I RECEIVED THIS HELP/SUPPORT...

APPLAUSE TO ME

ONE THING I DID TODAY I GIVE MYSELF APPLAUSE IS...

DAILY 9 REVIEW
VOWS FOR TOMORROW

01. For Enjoying Myself

I vow to spend 5 minutes more tomorrow enjoying…

_____

02. For Growing my knowledge

I vow to spend 5 minutes more tomorrow reading or listening…

_____

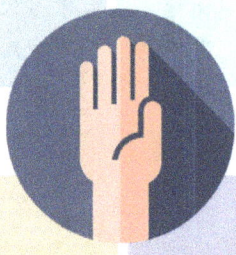

03. For Improving my Health

I vow to spend 5 minutes more tomorrow breaking one habit food or smoking or eating…

_____

04. For My compassion to others

I vow to spend 5 minutes more to praise or boost two friends …

_____

DAILY 10 PLAN
FOCUS ON SELF

	Minutes	✓

Morning

	Minutes	
Big Breathing with bell (R)	20	○
Gate Gate 15 (R)	15	○
Four Position Tongue Release (R)	1	○

Day

Mindful Walking (R)	5	○
Stress Reduction Count Breathing	As Needed	○
Instruction - How to's reading	10	○

Lunch - Mindful Eating (R) ○

Evening

Big Breathing 3 X Before Dinner   11   ○

Dinner - Eating Mindfully (R) ○

~Work Sheets~

Day 10 Plan	8	○
Spending-Wasting Time	5	○
My Good Day	2	○
Vow for Tomorrow	4	○

Bedtime

Gratitude Energy Meditation (R)	20	○
Comforting Vibe Mu, Vu, Ah (R)		

Total Time For Myself Today   /80   Total Circles Checked   _____

DAILY 10 REVIEW
SPENDING OR WASTING TIME

How I Spent My Time Today Date __/__/____	Time Wasted	Time Spent Well
Sleep		
Paid Work		
Eating - Cooking		
Personal Grooming		
Healthcare - Exercise - Sport		
Shopping - Errand - House Care		
Travel - Driving		
School - Education		
Group Friends - Social		
Individual Friends		
Family - Children - Partner		
Wellness - Yoga / Zen - Spiritual		
Personal Practices - Mindful / Read - Think - Hobby		
Social - Computer - Media - Games - Communication		
Entertainment - Movies - Theater - Live Music		
Caring for Others - Charity		
Quiet or Alone		
Total		

DAILY 10 PLAN
MY GOOD DAY

TODAY I MOST ENJOYED DOING...

TODAY I MOST ENJOYED SEEING/WATCHING...

TODAY I ENJOYED MYSELF WHEN...

TODAY I WAS AMAZED /PLEASED WHEN I RECEIVED THIS HELP/SUPPORT...

APPLAUSE TO ME

ONE THING I DID TODAY I GIVE MYSELF APPLAUSE IS...

DAILY 10 REVIEW
VOWS FOR TOMORROW

01. **For Enjoying Myself**

I vow to spend 5 minutes more tomorrow enjoying...

_____

02. **For Growing my knowledge**

I vow to spend 5 minutes more tomorrow reading or listening...

_____

03. **For Improving my Health**

I vow to spend 5 minutes more tomorrow breaking one habit food or smoking or eating...

_____

04. **For My compassion to others**

I vow to spend 5 minutes more to praise or boost two friends ...

_____

DAILY 11 PLAN
FOCUS ON SELF

	Minutes	✓

Morning
Big Breathing with bell (R)	20	○
Gate Gate 15 (R)	15	○
Four Position Tongue Release (R)	1	○

Day
Mindful Walking (R)	5	○
Stress Reduction Count Breathing	As Needed	○
Instruction - How to's reading	10	○

Lunch - Mindful Eating (R) ○

Evening

Big Breathing 3 X Before Dinner	11	○

Dinner - Eating Mindfully (R) ○

~Work Sheets~
Day 11 Plan	8	○
Spending-Wasting Time	5	○
My Good Day	2	○
Vow for Tomorrow	4	○

Bedtime
Gratitude Energy Meditation (R) Comforting Vibe Mu, Vu, Ah (R)	20	○

Total Time For Myself Today   /80   Total Circles Checked   _____

DAILY 11 REVIEW
SPENDING OR WASTING TIME

How I Spent My Time Today Date __/__/____	Time Wasted	Time Spent Well
Sleep		
Paid Work		
Eating - Cooking		
Personal Grooming		
Healthcare - Exercise - Sport		
Shopping - Errand - House Care		
Travel - Driving		
School - Education		
Group Friends - Social		
Individual Friends		
Family - Children - Partner		
Wellness - Yoga / Zen - Spiritual		
Personal Practices - Mindful / Read - Think - Hobby		
Social - Computer - Media - Games - Communication		
Entertainment - Movies - Theater - Live Music		
Caring for Others - Charity		
Quiet or Alone		
Total		

DAILY 11 PLAN
MY GOOD DAY

TODAY I MOST ENJOYED DOING...

TODAY I MOST ENJOYED SEEING/WATCHING...

TODAY I ENJOYED MYSELF WHEN...

TODAY I WAS AMAZED /PLEASED WHEN I RECEIVED THIS HELP/SUPPORT...

APPLAUSE TO ME

ONE THING I DID TODAY I GIVE MYSELF APPLAUSE IS...

DAILY 11 REVIEW
VOWS FOR TOMORROW

01. For Enjoying Myself

I vow to spend 5 minutes more tomorrow enjoying...

_____

02. For Growing my knowledge

I vow to spend 5 minutes more tomorrow reading or listening...

_____

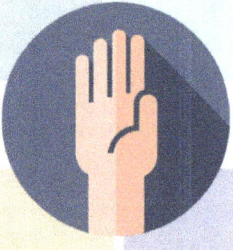

03. For Improving my Health

I vow to spend 5 minutes more tomorrow breaking one habit food or smoking or eating...

_____

04. For My compassion to others

I vow to spend 5 minutes more to praise or boost two friends ...

_____

DAILY 12 PLAN
FOCUS ON SELF

	Minutes	✓

Morning

	Minutes	
Big Breathing with bell (R)	20	○
Gate Gate 15 (R)	15	○
Four Position Tongue Release (R)	1	○

Day

Mindful Walking (R)	5	○
Stress Reduction Count Breathing	As Needed	○
Instruction - How to's reading	10	○

Lunch - Mindful Eating (R) ○

Evening

Big Breathing 3 X Before Dinner	11	○

Dinner - Eating Mindfully (R) ○

~Work Sheets~

Day 12 Plan	8	○
Spending-Wasting Time	5	○
My Good Day	2	○
Vow for Tomorrow	4	○

Bedtime

Gratitude Energy Meditation (R)	20	○
Comforting Vibe Mu, Vu, Ah (R)		

Total Time For Myself Today   /80   Total Circles Checked   _____

DAILY 12 REVIEW
SPENDING OR WASTING TIME

How I Spent My Time Today Date __/__/____	Time Wasted	Time Spent Well
Sleep		
Paid Work		
Eating - Cooking		
Personal Grooming		
Healthcare - Exercise - Sport		
Shopping - Errand - House Care		
Travel - Driving		
School - Education		
Group Friends - Social		
Individual Friends		
Family - Children - Partner		
Wellness - Yoga / Zen - Spiritual		
Personal Practices - Mindful / Read - Think - Hobby		
Social - Computer - Media - Games - Communication		
Entertainment - Movies - Theater - Live Music		
Caring for Others - Charity		
Quiet or Alone		
Total		

DAILY 12 PLAN
MY GOOD DAY

TODAY I MOST ENJOYED DOING...

TODAY I MOST ENJOYED SEEING/WATCHING...

TODAY I ENJOYED MYSELF WHEN...

TODAY I WAS AMAZED /PLEASED WHEN I RECEIVED THIS HELP/SUPPORT...

APPLAUSE TO ME

ONE THING I DID TODAY I GIVE MYSELF APPLAUSE IS...

DAILY 12 REVIEW
VOWS FOR TOMORROW

01. For Enjoying Myself

I vow to spend 5 minutes more tomorrow enjoying...

_____

02. For Growing my knowledge

I vow to spend 5 minutes more tomorrow reading or listening...

_____

03. For Improving my Health

I vow to spend 5 minutes more tomorrow breaking one habit food or smoking or eating...

_____

04. For My compassion to others

I vow to spend 5 minutes more to praise or boost two friends ...

_____

DAILY 13 PLAN
FOCUS ON SELF

	Minutes	✓

Morning
Big Breathing with bell (R)	20	○
Gate Gate 15 (R)	15	○
Four Position Tongue Release (R)	1	○

Day
Mindful Walking (R)	5	○
Stress Reduction Count Breathing	As Needed	○
Instruction - How to's reading	10	○

Lunch - Mindful Eating (R) ○

Evening
Big Breathing 3 X Before Dinner	11	○

Dinner - Eating Mindfully (R) ○

~Work Sheets~
Day 13 Plan	8	○
Spending-Wasting Time	5	○
My Good Day	2	○
Vow for Tomorrow	4	○

Bedtime
Gratitude Energy Meditation (R)	20	○
Comforting Vibe Mu, Vu, Ah (R)		

Total Time For Myself Today   /80   Total Circles Checked   _____

DAILY 13 REVIEW
SPENDING OR WASTING TIME

How I Spent My Time Today Date __/__/____	Time Wasted	Time Spent Well
Sleep		
Paid Work		
Eating - Cooking		
Personal Grooming		
Healthcare - Exercise - Sport		
Shopping - Errand - House Care		
Travel - Driving		
School - Education		
Group Friends - Social		
Individual Friends		
Family - Children - Partner		
Wellness - Yoga / Zen - Spiritual		
Personal Practices - Mindful / Read - Think - Hobby		
Social - Computer - Media - Games - Communication		
Entertainment - Movies - Theater - Live Music		
Caring for Others - Charity		
Quiet or Alone		
Total		

DAILY 13 PLAN
MY GOOD DAY

TODAY I MOST ENJOYED DOING...

TODAY I MOST ENJOYED SEEING/WATCHING...

TODAY I ENJOYED MYSELF WHEN...

TODAY I WAS AMAZED /PLEASED WHEN I RECEIVED THIS HELP/SUPPORT...

APPLAUSE TO ME

ONE THING I DID TODAY I GIVE MYSELF APPLAUSE IS...

DAILY 13 REVIEW
VOWS FOR TOMORROW

01. **For Enjoying Myself**

I vow to spend 5 minutes more tomorrow enjoying...

_____

02. **For Growing my knowledge**

I vow to spend 5 minutes more tomorrow reading or listening...

_____

03. **For Improving my Health**

I vow to spend 5 minutes more tomorrow breaking one habit food or smoking or eating...

_____

04. **For My compassion to others**

I vow to spend 5 minutes more to praise or boost two friends ...

_____

DAILY 14 PLAN
FOCUS ON SELF

	Minutes	✓

Morning

	Minutes	
Big Breathing with bell (R)	20	○
Gate Gate 15 (R)	15	○
Four Position Tongue Release (R)	1	○

Day

Mindful Walking (R)	5	○
Stress Reduction Count Breathing	As Needed	○
Instruction - How to's reading	10	○

Lunch - Mindful Eating (R) ○

Evening

Big Breathing 3 X Before Dinner	11	○

Dinner - Eating Mindfully (R) ○

~Work Sheets~

Day 14 Plan	8	○
Spending-Wasting Time	5	○
My Good Day	2	○
Vow for Tomorrow	4	○

Bedtime

Gratitude Energy Meditation (R)	20	○
Comforting Vibe Mu, Vu, Ah (R)		

Total Time For Myself Today   /80   Total Circles Checked   _____

DAILY 14 REVIEW
SPENDING OR WASTING TIME

How I Spent My Time Today Date __/__/____	Time Wasted	Time Spent Well
Sleep		
Paid Work		
Eating - Cooking		
Personal Grooming		
Healthcare - Exercise - Sport		
Shopping - Errand - House Care		
Travel - Driving		
School - Education		
Group Friends - Social		
Individual Friends		
Family - Children - Partner		
Wellness - Yoga / Zen - Spiritual		
Personal Practices - Mindful / Read - Think - Hobby		
Social - Computer - Media - Games - Communication		
Entertainment - Movies - Theater - Live Music		
Caring for Others - Charity		
Quiet or Alone		
Total		

DAILY 14 PLAN
MY GOOD DAY

TODAY I MOST ENJOYED DOING...

TODAY I MOST ENJOYED SEEING/WATCHING...

TODAY I ENJOYED MYSELF WHEN...

TODAY I WAS AMAZED /PLEASED WHEN I RECEIVED THIS HELP/SUPPORT...

👏 APPLAUSE TO ME 👏

ONE THING I DID TODAY I GIVE MYSELF APPLAUSE IS...

DAILY 14 REVIEW
VOWS FOR TOMORROW

01. For Enjoying Myself

I vow to spend 5 minutes more tomorrow enjoying...

_____

02. For Growing my knowledge

I vow to spend 5 minutes more tomorrow reading or listening...

_____

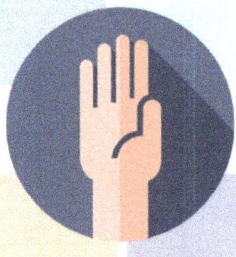

03. For Improving my Health

I vow to spend 5 minutes more tomorrow breaking one habit food or smoking or eating...

_____

04. For My compassion to others

I vow to spend 5 minutes more to praise or boost two friends ...

_____

4

New life. Fresh thinking.

You're changing why shouldn't your views change, too? Rethinking your view of life can improve your well-being. Fresh ideas may make things easier and offer more options than those you previously relied on.

Our early childhood influences have shaped our thinking, beliefs, and life strategies well into adulthood. But it wasn't perfect, was it? When you find the courage to question lifelong beliefs, your mind opens and the ground shakes.

Buddhists teach that all obstacles to happiness come from our thoughts. We are not born with a pre-existing philosophy of life or methods for living well. Our sense of well-being and satisfaction, our core life model is influenced by the foundational years of thought training.

But how can we let go of those ideas? How can we change thoughts and attitudes, especially when they're rooted in ineffective patterns?

Right now, we're living inside a thinking box. Everything we know about life and believe about ourselves exists within this box. It's been filled since our earliest days back when we were new and the box was empty.

But we were not empty. We were something. We existed. We weren't nothing. We had essence, spirit, and the presence of self. Our consciousness was blooming. That self wasn't troubled or broken. It had no doubts, no worries.

Everything now in our thought box has been accumulated since then. And these are the very obstructions we now struggle with

An open mind is essential for making fresh observations and processing new information effectively. It's important not to anticipate results, but to let new experiences unfold and be fully seen. A pre-determined mind is often a feature of unhappiness. Conditioned by misconceptions about causes and outcomes, this mind accepts false beliefs that block the path to success. Opening ourselves to new ideas reveals a new way forward.

The guide's daily practices enhance self-awareness and clarity, helping us observe our thoughts. This awareness encourages us to question childhood beliefs especially those that shape our self-image. As we expand our self-knowledge, we build self-trust, leading to wiser decisions based on current reality. Releasing outdated ideas just long enough to unblock the mind allows us to create refreshing and empowering life strategies for the present

Designed for success

We were born to succeed, but sometimes life throws us a curveball. Early childhood conditioning may have introduced bugs and malware into our natural success system, infecting the most perfect mechanism ever created. But we are no longer children we now have the freedom to challenge our lives and expect success. We can cleanse our systems of these bugs and malware, restoring the powerful force that drives us forward. This success system remains intact and undamaged.

Humans are the greatest competitors on Earth, naturally equipped to succeed and thrive. Success and happiness are hardwired into us. By living consciously, we allow this internal system to function as it was intended to self-heal and guide us. Even if it was disrupted in childhood, when there was neither space nor time to heal, it can now be restored to full power. We must trust in the innate technology of being human. With mindful living, that trust is rewarded, enabling us to reclaim our birthright to succeed.

When bugs do arise, they're defeated before they can harm your success software. You begin to seek out pressure situations. You meet your moment of truth and triumph.

There's no grief, no trauma, no crisis Too great for you to handle because you were designed to succeed and to survive and to thrive.

Success is part of your very DNA it's what made humans the greatest competitors on Earth. We have an inherent potential to succeed and thrive. No amount of early abuse or neglect can erase the fact that success and winning are our birthrights. Our survival systems are designed to operate in crises and emergencies. Succeeding is what humans do best.

There is no grief, no trauma, no crisis too great for you to process because you were designed to triumph overall. You've already gone through so much and may doubt yourself because things haven't worked out as planned. You may wonder, What's wrong with me? You may be experiencing an emotional crisis right now, in this very moment, and thinking, how am I going to get through this? You'll get through it by relying on the success systems you were born with systems that are still within you.

If we were born to achieve, what went wrong? Somewhere along the way, we picked up infectious bugs and malware in our once-pristine operating systems. Early childhood conditions may have introduced these infections, disrupting our success systems and causing dysfunction. It's common for these natural systems to be interrupted, leading to issues in adulthood depression, anxiety, phobias, addictions. Even our physical health can suffer.

But we are no longer children. We don't have to live under the influence of those infected emotional defenses from our past. We still possess the most powerful winning nature in the known universe.

We can cleanse our operating systems of outdated childhood survival strategies like emotional repression and avoidance. These are cancers to the adult system. Our highly effective programming endures let's restore the brilliance that has been buried. As adults, we now have something children don't: the freedom to challenge our lives and to hope. We also have 2,600 years of Buddhist practices and principles to guide us. These healing principles are embedded in the daily plans.

This restorative process works on both the conscious and subconscious levels.

While childhood trauma or life's arrows may have left deep wounds, the present moment offers both the space and time to heal. Use these two weeks wisely to reconnect with your original, best self. Commit to the daily plan and workbooks to liberate both your mind and body, empowering you to live a life filled with joy, optimism, and unshackled potential.

Breathing for happiness

Your breathing system is imprinted with your emotional personality as if it has a personality of its own. Are you generally happy or often sad? Do you spend much of your time worrying and feeling fearful, or are you naturally optimistic and hopeful? When we change how we breathe, we shift our emotional state. As our emotional baseline changes, so does our outlook on life. This is a key reason why the activities in this program are so transformative.

Has anyone ever told you that your breathing sounds sad? Or said, "You seem to be breathing very happily today"? It might sound ridiculous, but breathing patterns actually influence parts of your personality. This happens because our emotions have been tied to how we breathe since childhood, forming either helpful or harmful breathing habits. The emotional-breathing connection established early in life continues into adulthood, often recreating the emotional landscape of our younger years. If your childhood was positive, your breathing likely supports that well-being. But if your early years were painful or traumatic, how might your breathing be limiting your happiness now?

It's not news that there's a connection between breathing and emotions but breathing as its own emotional personality? That's something most people don't consider. Breathing isn't just a response to emotions it also creates them. We're often told to "take a deep breath and relax" or simply "breathe" in stressful moments. Watch a child and you'll see how erratic their breathing becomes when crying or excited. Likewise, an angry adult might hold their breath until their face changes color just like a child.

So how can we use breathing not only to cope better under stress, but to cultivate a more positive, emotionally resilient personality? The answer lies in reprogramming our breathing patterns.

Your breathing personality influences your emotional state even more than your thoughts do. If you were a sad or anxious child, your breathing encoded that experience. If you were happy and secure, your breath supports that. Emotional conditioning from childhood formed as your brain developed is now etched into your physical breathing system.

Every breath you take reinforces both the best and the most challenging aspects of your formative years. With around 7,000 breaths a day, your body silently sings the song of your childhood emotions. If your early foundation was fearful and uncertain, today's breathing patterns may trigger those same feelings. If that foundation was safe and loving, your breath carries that too. Optimism or pessimism didn't begin with thought—it began with breath.

Take a look at your current emotional state. How do you respond to life's inevitable ups and downs? If you want to heal from an unhappy childhood, focus on improving your current state of mind which is still being shaped by the physical act of breathing. You don't need to reconstruct the past; it lives on in your breath. Whatever your emotional personality is, it's being reinforced, day and night, with every breath.

And it's more powerful than thought. Our breath-body, imprinted during brain development, is designed to override conscious thinking. Though we've grown, our breathing instrument may still be playing the tune of the past—breath by breath, shaping our emotions and worldview.

But here's the good news: this automatic imprint can be overwritten. Because breathing is both involuntary and voluntary, conscious breathing practices like those in this program can restore your system's natural rhythm. And with that rhythm comes your original emotional design: love and confidence.

Breathe better, feel happier.

Breathing, power of survival.

The respiratory system is a key component of human survival, engineered to function independently of conscious thought and willpower. It harnesses some of the most formidable forces within human nature to ensure our survival.

People often wonder: Why can't I overcome my sadness? Why can't I be a better version of myself? What's wrong with me? I've accomplished a lot, I'm very smart, and I've disciplined myself in many areas, yet I can't control my impulses or my thinking to make my life happier and more productive.

The answer lies in the fact that the survival system is designed to win. It's the strongest force in human nature, so even brilliant thinking and strong willpower cannot override it during times of stress. Under stress, it will always overpower conscious thought, as it is meant to do. However, breathing is the one component of this system we can control.

Breathing, as part of the survival system, isn't your enemy. Your intelligence and willpower can be effective under stress, but they won't work if your breathing pattern was damaged when it served as your childhood's last line of defense against unbearable situations. What was effective for a child no longer suits the adult. Through voluntary control of our breath, we can reshape the breathing-emotional program that influences our temperament and personality.

Breathing is both autonomous and voluntary. No other autonomous function possesses this duality. We can't alter our heartbeats, control dopamine or adrenaline, or influence any other survival-related response. The ability to regulate our breathing, however, is one of the most powerful tools for improving our emotional state. By consciously controlling the speed, depth, and rhythm of our breathing, we can override the involuntary, habitual operations that govern our responses. In doing so, we reset the program, altering our reactions to stress and life events. This also leads to a shift in our temperament and outlook on life. Without this conscious effort, nothing will fundamentally change in how we respond to stress.

Scientific evidence shows that breath timing is controlled by a few thousand neurons in the brain. Through mindful and conscious breathing techniques, we can clear these neurons of 'bugs' and 'malware,' restoring our healthy breathing system. This, in turn, frees us from negative and harmful emotional states and reprograms our breathing to promote a calmer, more content emotional state. By regulating our breathing instrument, we also make positive adjustments to our thinking and emotions.

The best way perhaps the only way we can control panic and anxiety is through breath control. Since the physical act of breathing is closely linked to our emotional wellbeing, we can transition from dissatisfaction to contentment, reduce panic to mild fear, and shift from depression to temporary sadness. Where we once had no power and could only react, reprogramming our breathing practices now enables us to regain control over confused thinking and harmful behavior.

Toxic breathing

Your breathing may be toxic to you. If you are struggling with disorders such as anxiety, depression, addiction, or phobia, it's likely that your breath is reinforcing these states. Breathing can become poisonous, contributing to emotional illness. How does something as essential as breathing become toxic? As a key component of the human survival system, breathing helps children survive emotional pain and fear by repressing emotions. This, however, was not the system's original design. In the abnormal, confined environment of childhood, repression provided some relief, helping the child endure prolonged emotional distress. Breathing as a means of emotional repression is the last defense of childhood the only relief. What was once a helpful form of repression for the child becomes poison for the adult.

Nature's method of repressing emotions is by tensing the body, especially the breathing muscles. For the child, repression of emotional sensations was the only viable option, as all other emotional defenses proved ineffective. This ultimate defense against torturous childhood conditions becomes embedded in the adult psyche. Yet, this repression is toxic to living a contented and satisfying life. It leads to emotional afflictions and addictive coping mechanisms. The emotionally scarred adult often finds that what was once natural breathing is now impossible. Damaged breathing becomes their new norm, and they remain unaware that it needs to be "rebooted." Breathing needs to be relearned and reprogrammed.

Growing up with tension and repression is like having a python wrapped around the chest and abdomen, inhibiting normal breathing. Though it alleviates the intensity of pain, it also numbs all other emotions. This was not a conscious choice but rather an instinctive response to a toxic environment. It was a matter of either repressing or enduring agonizing fear and pain. As the child matured into adulthood, holding their breath and remaining tense became habitual. This habit perpetuates the pain, confusion, and fear rooted in childhood trauma. This toxic defensive pattern denies the adult's ability to fully experience emotions. Particularly under stress or excitement, it suppresses the adult just as it did the child. Their emotional state is dominated by fear and trauma. Though the adult is no longer the confined child, they remain trapped by their breathing patterns, cycling through thousands of breaths every day.

Breathing as healing

The breath has amazing power for healing as it does for toxicity. With one mindful breath we begin to heal because it is a direct path to our automatic responses. We can free ourselves of our troublesome thoughts by focusing on our breathing. We cease reinforcing the loneliness and unworthiness we may have experienced as children. By focusing on our breath, we create space between our spinning 40,000 thoughts and our deep, peaceful self. With just one full, fluid breath we go from repressed to expressed, from closed to open, and from self-hate to self-love. It is that powerful as an instrument of change. It is our human technology which is functioning. The challenge is not one breath but the 7000 we take every day.

Years of negative and harmful patterns can be reprogrammed, overcoming depression, anxiety, and phobias. Personality and spirit will be uplifted. Life strategies and views will grow. Normal, healthy breathing creates a flowing, happy emotional state. Life becomes fuller and contented as conscious breathing practices help regulate intense emotional situations. No stress is too great when using breathing as a tool. Even in situations of panic, with the correct breathing practices, it is possible to leverage the panic response to improve physical and mental capabilities.

In this way, mindful breathing is not only for healing but also for thriving. Maintaining optimal breathing allows us to control our impulses under stressful situations for functioning at our best, not our worst. By learning to breathe fully and deeply, we create space for our feelings rather than squeezing them.

The snake lets go, and our healthy breathing system restores. Breathing well opens life's channels for a full emotional-sensory flow, delivering a rich and nourishing life experience. Breathing practice nurtures emotional well-being while promoting mental calm and clarity.

The daily plan includes these techniques, which anchor you in stressful times by restoring optimal breathing. You become more present in each moment, more peaceful, and unshakably connected to your confident self. The plan becomes a practice for maintaining emotional-breath health, similar to going to the gym to build strength and maintain physical health. We don't build muscle in one visit, nor do we transform our life with a single breath. What we are doing is transforming a lifetime of toxic breath back to its full and fluid function. The goal is to be healing and renewing ourselves, even while sleeping, when our breathing is involuntary.

Become a master of your breath in every situation. Commit to well-being by practicing breath-awareness in the daily plan. Allow for the expression and acceptance of all emotions. You can express and embrace emotions that your child was unable to. This promotes a deeper connection with ourselves and with those closest to us. Restoring our breathing system and learning to breathe deeply, without our old friend, the snake, squeezing the life from us, we will feel fully and love wholeheartedly.

The 3 laws of emotion.

> The three laws of emotions apply to everything you feel. Without these laws, following a daily program or any mindful practice would be of little benefit. When you follow the daily program, it will promote emotional healing effortlessly. It's like an apple falling from a tree; it happens every time as a result of the natural law of gravity. By following the program, you can't help but feel better.
>
> These laws govern the perception of emotions, how to calm disturbing emotions, and the origins of these emotions. Many common beliefs about emotional sensations conflict with these laws and actually reduce their effectiveness. One such belief is, "If you think better, you will feel

better." This stems from the idea that most emotions are simply in your head. Another common belief is that emotions need to be controlled or managed. This also hinders the natural laws of emotions from working as they are designed to promote health and happiness.

First law of emotion.

The first law of emotion is that emotions are sensory. They exist in your body and are perceived in your mind as sensations. The mind labels and assigns value, but it doesn't create them. According to this law, the sensory nature of emotions means that the body reacts to physical and sensory stimuli. If we are yelled at or attacked, we respond with a sensation that is processed in the mind. It's not the mind generating the sensations; it is only classifying them. Consequently, we can't raise our emotional IQ or well-being through a purely mental approach. It is the sensory body that controls our emotional well-being more profoundly than the mind.

In the mind, emotions are classified, and value is either added or subtracted. How this is done depends on conditional factors: culture, age, prejudice, gender, and so on. There are no absolutes or universal agreements on how to label these sensations. There is no A equals B; emotional experiences do not cause one to react with pain, joy, sadness, or happiness in a fixed manner.

Sensory emotions exist in their own right, without any thinking or judgment. They are as they are, like sunlight or rain. Classifying them doesn't change or enrich them in any way it actually diminishes them. All mental labels degrade the enjoyment and satisfaction we naturally derive from them. Why label them at all? By sensing our emotions without labeling, judging, or explaining them, we uncover and appreciate our deeper truth.

The second law of emotion.

The second law of emotion suggests that there are no inherent emotions. We label sensory experiences as emotions, but these are simply arbitrary names. What one culture calls love, another may call lust. In some places, depression was once labeled as melancholy. According to Buddhism, there are no pure emotions no bad or good emotions. Everything we call an emotion is merely the result of our trained minds interpreting bodily experiences.

When we label our emotional sensations, we are constructing a philosophy about life. If we experience an excited sensation, do we call it fear, or do we embrace it? If we lived in a different time, country, or culture, our minds would interpret our emotional sensations through that lens. Happiness might refer to a different state, and sorrow might hold a different meaning. In Buddhism, death is not seen with sorrow. We mentally name, explain, categorize, and even blame our emotions. According to our minds, there are noble and sinful emotions. And therein lies the source of our trouble with emotions believing our minds are the ultimate authority.

Labeling sensations as specific emotions can be limiting. It is more beneficial to experience these emotional sensations without assigning labels, although it is understandable that we often need to communicate with others. Discussing emotions can be challenging without terms like "the sensation I am experiencing, which I previously identified as love" or "the anger I call 'anger,' which makes me want to fight." Therefore, for practical communication, we use labels for these sensations. However, if you want to fully experience love or anger, it's best not to label it. Instead, observe these sensations without classifying them. This will give you a truer understanding of your experience, offering a much fuller emotional journey.

When green is not green.

Think of it this way: if I ask you to describe the color green, you can't do it. If I ask you to show me the color green, you might pick out a plant let's say it's a tree. But when we look closely, we can't see two leaves with exactly the same tone and intensity. Every leaf is green, yet none are alike. There's no single green we can use to define all others. And even if there were a uniform green, thinking and saying "green" limits our experience of seeing the tree and its wonderful variety of greens. We're thinking about it instead of truly experiencing it. As soon as we say "green," or "leaf," or even "tree," we are trying to think through our experience. Self-limiting.

Love is like leaves. Aside from communication, why would we try to define it? Naming our feelings of love reduces the depth of our emotions to a shallow cartoon. Any label is thinking about the emotion instead of experiencing it. If you want a full understanding or the full impact of emotions, the better approach is to experience the sensations without thinking or mental interference. Just see it for what it is and experience it.

Many are quick to label their feelings. It's a control and avoidance mechanism for managing uncomfortable emotions. And by uncomfortable, I mean any emotion including love and joy. By labeling them as soon as they arise, we shift from our bodies to our heads, disconnecting from the full experience. How much better it is to sit quietly with our emotional sensations. We can always classify them later. Enjoy them. Give them their full weight and allow them time to rise and fall.

We place so much emphasis on unhappiness, sadness, and all these emotional labels. We spend so much time dissecting love, hate, depression, and anger because we're trying to solve what we perceive as a mental problem with a mental solution. But the emotional issues we think we have are rooted in sensory experience, and so is the remedy. We must first take a sensory, experiential approach to emotional health.

In any case, there are no pure sensations or emotions. Love is blended with excitement and curiosity. Anger may be laced with frustration and fear. Pain cannot be quantified or described, only its intensity can be labeled. When we label sensations, we allow our minds to lead us instead of our true sensory awareness. Labels approximate our feelings, and may be helpful for communication, but they are mere approximations of the experience of living. Emotional truth lives in our raw sensory flow, where all emotions exist moment by moment together, inseparable rising and falling, dissolving and being renewed.

The third law of emotion.

The third law of emotions is that emotions only exist in the present moment. They do not reside in the fabrications of time, the past and the future, any more than we can live in the past or the future. So, why is so much emotional therapy invested in reliving the past? You can relive the past all you want, but you'll never change it. And while you can understand why your memory of the past may be disturbing, it's the sensory emotional flow in the present moment that needs attention. It's because the sensory emotional flow is misunderstood that so much effort is put into mental reconstructions of the past.

Flowing emotions are life-giving. There is no time to life, but there is this flow of life. There is only this flow of the moment. The more sensations we can experience in each moment, the more time we have, because the moments are richer. The moment is always moving, always changing, and we move with it. I like the way the Buddhists put it: one can't put their toe in the river at the same place twice. We cannot relive any emotion from any time in our past, no matter how traumatic or how wonderful. But we can live the pure truth of our sensory emotional flow.

Flowing emotions are healing, and all emotions are flowing all the time. We don't get stuck in anger, trauma, or depression. We get stuck in our mental interpretations of these (what is fondly called memory). We recall past events in the present moment with our thoughts. A memory from the past is a reimagined experience, and an imagined experience does create sensory-emotions, so we think we have emotions from the past. However, it's the present moment we're experiencing. The only way to resolve disturbing emotions is to deal with the sensory emotional flow now.

The river of emotional sensations is always flowing through us, invigorating, changing, and unfolding with each and every moment. It's a natural healing system. All is impermanent in the world, and emotions are the same. Disturbing or unpleasant emotional sensations arise and fade according to the value and weight they merit. Grief, sadness, anger, pain—these dissolve themselves in the perfect manner of a cloud, always moving, ever changing form. The same is true for pleasing sensory feelings like joy and happiness; nothing is permanent. This is our universal truth, so why would one think emotions are different? No one is destined to be in a permanent emotional state, but many think they are.

Then why do we suffer? Why does agony and distress linger and overwhelm us if the sensory flow is self-healing? Sometimes, humans are under prolonged, severe stress, and the only relief comes from shutting down this sensory flow with physical tension. Children repress this stream after all other options for comfort are exhausted. Repressing sensory-emotional flow with body and breath tension, although necessary, was not normal. When emotions aren't allowed to flow, all senses are repressed. Physical repression agitates sensory-emotions and creates a persistent emotional state. Tension is like carrying a weight on your back day and night. It wouldn't be helpful to a happy, go-lucky personality, would it? Under prolonged conditions, this repressed state becomes the new normal, well into adulthood. And so, we suffer. The emotional flow, our natural healing system, has been restricted and damaged.

We can restore our natural healing system and nurture it through a combination of relaxation and concentration practices as outlined in the daily program and recordings. When following the plan, repressed childhood sensations and emotions may arise. That's progress. The adult should give these feelings the time they require, trusting that they will fade, though they once overwhelmed the vulnerable child. The learned reaction is to avoid them. It requires courage to fight the child's survival impulse to immediately repress disturbing feelings and, instead, allow them to flow. Increasingly, with observation of this healing process, these feelings will dissolve and begin to flow, healing, as they are designed to do

Childhood Bugs and Malware

If you can't be as happy as you think you deserve to be, the roots may lie in your childhood. No child is born with persistent unhappiness. Babies and toddlers don't start life with worries or anxieties. The natural state of children is one of love and happiness carefree, trusting, and secure in their environment. When the environment doesn't provide the security a child expects, it stirs fear. This fear creates emotional "bugs" and "malware" like low self-esteem, anxiety, and fear.

An abnormally insecure environment isn't just dysfunctional, it's absolute torture. If you feel empty or unsure about the direction of your life, or if you're dealing with depression, anxiety, trauma, addiction, or other issues, take a moment to trace your past. And by "trace," I don't mean following the conventional wisdom of simply revisiting the events of your childhood. Instead, I mean examine your reactions and responses to your childhood environment.

I'm not suggesting that merely tracing your past will resolve these issues. Knowing what happened, even if you think you fully understand it, isn't the solution to your problems.

Caterpillar and butterfly.

Survival is the only purpose critical to a baby, toddler, and child. This powerful survival force within the child is life itself, yet it remains as mystifying to adults as a caterpillar is to a butterfly. We can't imagine the intensity of this force within children. It also challenges us to understand how this purpose shapes our adult behaviors and life strategies. The strangest part is that it doesn't matter that we survived, but rather how we survived impacts our adult lives.

The first and most fundamental necessity is attachment to the caregiver be it the parents or the family. Attachment creates safety and soothes the survival system. Children aren't designed to emerge from the womb and immediately run from tigers and lions. They are entirely dependent. If a child doesn't feel attached to their caregivers, they won't feel safe and will do everything they can to create and maintain attachment and a sense of security. How long can a child survive without care? Children need to feel attached and safe every hour of every day.

You may say, "Well, I had a loving family" or "Everything was good in my family." You may feel you cannot think anything bad about the people who gave you life. But it's not what your parents did. It's not about love, food, or shelter—not precisely. It's how you reacted to the environment. The problem causing stress may not have been the caregivers themselves; it may have been external stresses like financial problems, conflict between the adults, or even war zones. A child has the right to feel everything they feel, regardless of the environment. When a child's emotions are acknowledged, they gain a sense of themselves and feel worthy. If they didn't feel safe, or if you didn't feel safe, it's still your truth. It cannot be disputed. It wasn't the child's choice to feel insecure, yet it is their reality.

The survival system always operates at high intensity when a child isn't comforted, feels neglected, or is insecure. The baby, toddler, and child will try every strategy possible from crying to yelling to being sweet and smiling to get the attachment and comfort they need to feel safe. When all else fails, the ultimate strategy is to use fear to intensify and attract attention, seeking comfort. When that doesn't work, pain takes over and exaggerates all the efforts to gain attention and comfort.

More and more, fear and pain become the child's norm. But no child can live every second of every day and night, every month, every year, with the unbearable suffering created by the most powerful force in human nature: the survival system. What strategy is left for the child to combat this agonizing fear and pain? All efforts toward attachment and safety have failed to provide comfort. The only tactic left for the child is to shut down and avoid the emotions and circumstances that confine them.

Avoidance as tactic.

How do we shut down and avoid our emotions? We do it through tension. Tensing our bodies reduces sensory awareness, allowing us to cope with pain and discomfort a little more easily. We tense ourselves all the time. When we get an injection, we tense our arm. If we have a broken bone fixed, we grit our teeth and brace ourselves. And in the dentist's chair well, it's not even a chair. It's more like a bed. Because if it were a chair, we'd be kicking doctors out the door as we react to the pain.

Long-term tension, however, wasn't designed for childhood. Childhood wasn't meant to carry the weight of agonizing emotions. Yet, the child lives in this state every minute, every day, and every night. This is the opposite of how the survival system is supposed to function. Relaxation, not tension, is the key to responding to emergencies and stressful situations. But that only works when a person is free to act.

Any person adult or child when confined and under extreme stress, will shut down their emotional disturbance and discomfort. However, when this becomes a long-term pattern, as in childhood, it creates a persistent, damaged condition that continues into adulthood as their emotional management method. Using a broken childhood system will not support a healthy life.

Minimizing and avoiding our emotions can harm our well-being by obstructing the natural flow of feelings. Although it reduces fear and pain, it leads to confusion in our emotional state. To be balanced and happy, we need a full emotional and sensory flow. If we are programmed with tension, we live confined by past patterns. We must clear these issues to achieve remarkable results. This is the goal of the daily plan.

Lost childhood, rediscovered self.

Cleaning our survival system of bugs and malware restores it to its natural state. This involves simple, mindful practices. Breathing techniques work with our human technology to restore freedom and fluidity in our breath. By developing deep concentration, we eliminate tension. Buddhists teach that a focused mind is free of tension, and this is our ideal. Living consciously in each moment connects us to our bodies and creates space from conditioned thinking. Fear and pain dissolve, leaving behind inner peace and self-love. We cannot restore the childhood we've lost, but we can restore our original programming, designed for living our best life.

Survival system

Your survival system is the strongest force in human nature. It has made humanity the greatest competitor on Earth. It is designed to override thinking and willpower, so people act in emergencies when life and death are on the line. The adrenaline rush, the dopamine: all of it makes us bigger, stronger, faster, and tougher in critical moments. So, why isn't it working for you now? Why can't you use your will and intellect to overcome self-destructive behaviors and create habits to be your best self?

In fact, it's working against you because its ultimate purpose has been damaged. Everything else in the survival system everything from childhood to adulthood is subconscious and automatic, except for breathing.

You might wonder, why can't I overcome my habits and self-defeating behaviors? I'm not dumb, I have willpower. I've accomplished things in life, yet I seem to disappoint myself over and over. The survival system isn't ruled by intelligence or willpower. It's a subconscious system, reacting automatically to stress. When it takes over, not even Einstein's intellect or Hercules's willpower can control it.

But when that survival system is damaged, we need to do what we can to clean out the bugs and malware in the parts of the system we have voluntary control over the breathing instrument.

No matter how poorly you feel about your life right now, be assured it is still within you. It's in your DNA. It's in the essence of who you are.

You don't have the wisdom to fix it because nothing is stronger than the survival system. Designed into our DNA, in our humanness, it was meant to override thinking, so we don't harm ourselves in life-and-death situations. But this system was damaged in childhood. I can explain how it was damaged, why it was damaged, and the things we did to try to overcome it. However, the good news is I know how to fix it. The only part of the survival system we can voluntarily control is breathing because breathing is both automatic and voluntary.

Breathing is also automatic when it's working well, but when it's damaged, it doesn't work for us.It works against us, but the good news is because it's voluntary, we can reprogram, in a sense, the breathing mechanism. We reprogram that breathing mechanism and what happens is you become confident, you become calm, you become clear-headed, you become empowered with your willpower and your wisdom.

Surviving childhood. Thriving adulthood

When you understand the relationship between childhood trauma, a dysfunctional environment, and role tension, it becomes clear. You are struggling with a force more powerful than your intellect and willpower. Your survival system resides in your body, and your body is designed to overpower your mind in order to ensure your survival. This is the most powerful force in human nature, and in many ways, it is beyond comprehension. It cannot be resolved through thought alone. The most powerful tool we have is relaxation

Sensations, programming our childhood

Nearly all the formative experiences of the baby, toddler, and young child were sensory experiences. The child learned through direct experience, not through thought, being told, reading books, or watching TV. Information that shaped their worldview was absorbed through sensory interaction. If we aim to transform harmful, detrimental, or traumatic experiences, doesn't it make sense that the only way to achieve this is through a sensory, experiential method? We cannot expect to help the child or the adult repair those childhood experiences solely with better thinking or increased awareness. While such realizations may offer benefit under normal life circumstances, when under stress, the adult will likely revert to the same sensory experiences and reactions they had in childhood. They will instinctively use the same childhood defense mechanisms to handle stress sensory defenses, like shutting down and repressing emotions. These were the only defenses available to the child during that time.

There is no new idea that can resolve this issue. You can search the internet for the most ancient wisdom or seek out the most brilliant minds of our time, but no idea will help you overcome your childhood defense mechanisms of repression and avoidance. These defenses were built upon a damaged survival system, relying on sensory input. They must be addressed and resolved in the same way.

Anything learned in childhood, when the mind was still developing, is imprinted deeply. The child, with thousands more neural receptors and heightened sensitivity to their environment, absorbed everything in order to maximize their chances of survival. This imprinting continues into adulthood, and the system operates as designed. But when you combine that early sensitivity and imprinting with the most powerful force in humankind the survival instinct you can see the challenge in overcoming any childhood damage. The hope for transforming this damage lies only within the sensory and survival systems themselves.

Intellectual approaches to healing and transformation are destined to fail. Sensory, experiential methods and techniques are the only true path to transforming a dysfunctional, troubled childhood into a fully functional and vibrant adulthood. So, isn't it somewhat ludicrous to think we can heal the sensations that hurt us as children with just an idea? You've experienced stress since you were a baby. Even as an infant, you could sense the tension from a dysfunctional family. Stress and anxiety were constant every second, every minute, every day, every week, throughout all the years of your childhood. This stress has been infecting your natural program, your true self.

Your behavior may be influenced by past trauma. Feelings of depression and anxiety often stem from difficult childhood experiences that affected your innate survival instincts. As children, you couldn't escape or fight back, so you repressed pain and fear by tensing your body and restricting your breath.

This repression can lead to emotional numbness, limiting your ability to fully experience life and connect with others. You might struggle with abandonment issues seeking love yet finding it difficult to accept when it's offered. The key to healing lies in opening up your body and releasing the built-up tension through conscious breathing.

Breathing exercises can help you process emotions naturally, preventing negative feelings like anger from escalating into rage or sadness from turning into depression. This approach allows you to live with clarity and authenticity, free from the constraints of past defenses. Ultimately, we all seek love and acceptance. Learning to breathe through intense emotions is crucial for overcoming deep-seated issues and reclaiming a sense of normalcy.

Childhood Stress Coping Mechanisms

Early childhood stress and trauma can have lasting effects on an adult's emotional and psychological well-being. Many people experience stress from a young age, especially in challenging environments. This early stress can deeply affect a person's sense of identity and responses to various situations, leading to long-term issues like anxiety, feelings of abandonment, and difficulty forming healthy relationships.

When children experience stress particularly in situations where they feel trapped and unable to escape, confront, or communicate their needs they often develop coping mechanisms to shield themselves from pain. These may include tensing their bodies and breath to suppress emotions and sensations. While these survival techniques can minimize fear and pain, they also hinder the ability to fully engage in life. The result is a complex emotional state that carries into adulthood.

Love Intimacy.

Love intimacy begins with loving yourself. Loving yourself isn't something that's "done" or earned; it's a natural state we're born with. Look at children in the playground, and you can see their excitement and confidence for life. You hear their laughter, giggles, and joyful shouts. Children who are loved and nourished act as though the world is made for them. They believe they can do no wrong. Whatever they do will be acknowledged, guided, and nurtured. They are full of love for themselves and the world around them.

We all possess this inborn love, whether we feel it or not. When childhood is filled with insecurity, neglect, or abuse, children repress their natural love, becoming apologetic and distrustful. They never experience what it feels like to be loved, how to love, or how to accept love. Yet, this natural loving state remains within all of us, and it cannot be erased.

For intimate love, we need to experience our own self-love and learn how to share it and accept it from others. When we love ourselves, there is no fear of rejection. There is no anger. We don't place our love and self-worth in the hands of others. We feel confident in our own love, so if others don't love us, we don't blame ourselves. We're not trying to heal the love we didn't receive from our parents or caretakers. Without fear, we are able to accept love openly and give love unconditionally.

Intimacy requires embracing all parts of yourself. Embrace your worries, fears, panic, and anxiety on one hand, and on the other, embrace your joy, bliss, and excitement for life. Accept that you're lovable even with your blemishes and deficiencies. Accept that others are also imperfect. It requires letting go of obstructions deeply rooted tensions and long-held beliefs about yourself. It requires the courage to experience hurt and not view the pain as a flaw. It requires the bravery to enter love without deception and to accept love as it is.

When one connects with their true loving nature, they naturally attract others who are also self-loving. When two people who love themselves come together, they share each other's love, rejoicing in one another. They mirror each other's best selves, and the image is joyful. There is no fear or jealousy. Each person's imperfections are accepted, as they accept their own. Intimacy is impossible when one is searching for self-love in another. Nor can another restore love that was denied in childhood. But by releasing long-held pain and suffering, healing follows, and self-love arises.

The Power of Silence

The rarest of the rare is silence. To be quiet within oneself is a kind of truth. In this truth, we find purpose and meaning. Silence quiets our thoughts and ideas. When we find ourselves enveloped in silence, we become one with it, shedding the weight of worry.

Here, our sensory perceptions exist without labels, creating a flawless experience. There is no beauty and no ugliness. There is no anger or joy only contentment and peace. It is a space free of judgment or explanation.

Many people have encountered this natural human phenomenon of inner silence without even realizing it. They have experienced moments of profound calm and unity with the world. During these times, there are no divisions or distractions. However, few individuals remain in silence long enough to truly encounter their authentic selves.

Why have we become so separated from this deep, quiet state, when all that is required of us is to practice tranquility? Buddhists say it is our monkey mind and its 40,000 daily thoughts that creates the noise we find so hard to escape. Silencing this monkey mind is essential to attaining peace.

Think of silence as the art of watching a sunset without judgment, listening to the earth's sounds without distraction, being profoundly present within oneself while time moves on.

In our fast-paced world, where distractions are abundant and noise seems inescapable, it is crucial for our well-being to take a step back and allow the world to pass by. We often need to quiet the clamor of daily life and make space to acknowledge our deepest needs connection, understanding, fulfillment, and inner peace.

The rush and chaos of our routines drown out these necessities, causing us to overlook what truly replenishes and nurtures our spirit. By intentionally silencing distractions and creating room for reflection, we cultivate a deeper sense of self-awareness and appreciation for our true natuThe rarest of the rare is silence. To be quiet within oneself is a kind of truth. In this truth, we find purpose and meaning. Silence quiets our thoughts and ideas. When we find ourselves enveloped in silence, we become one with it, shedding the weight of worry.

Here, our sensory perceptions exist without labels, creating a flawless experience. There is no beauty and no ugliness. There is no anger or joy only contentment and peace. It is a space free of judgment or explanation.

Many people have encountered this natural human phenomenon of inner silence without even realizing it. They have experienced moments of profound calm and unity with the world. During these times, there are no divisions or distractions. However, few individuals remain in silence long enough to truly encounter their authentic selves.

Why have we become so separated from this deep, quiet state, when all that is required of us is to practice tranquility? Buddhists say it is our monkey mind and its 40,000 daily thoughts that create the noise we find so hard to escape. Silencing this monkey mind is essential to attaining peace.

Think of silence as the art of watching a sunset without judgment, listening to the earth's sounds without distraction, being profoundly present within oneself while time moves on.

In our fast-paced world, where distractions are abundant and noise seems inescapable, it is crucial for our well-being to take a step back and allow the world to pass by. We often need to quiet the clamor of daily life and make space to acknowledge our deepest needs connection, understanding, fulfillment, and inner peace.

The rush and chaos of our routines drown out these necessities, causing us to overlook what truly replenishes and nurtures our spirit. By intentionally silencing distractions and creating room for reflection, we cultivate a deeper sense of self-awareness and appreciation for our true nature.

Why Silence is Essential

Reconnecting with Your Inner Self

By embracing silence, we can reconnect with our inner selves, understanding our fears, joys, aspirations, and anxieties. This introspection is vital for personal growth and helps us identify what truly nourishes our spirit.

1. Cultivating Gratitude: In moments of silence, we can reflect on the blessings in our lives, cultivating a sense of gratitude. Recognizing and appreciating the nourishment we receive from relationships, nature, creativity, and even simple moments of joy can enhance our overall well-being. Gratitude also fosters the present moment the only place where gratitude exists.

2. Enhancing Focus and Clarity: Silencing the mind allows us to regain focus. When we are not bombarded by constant noise, we can think more clearly, make better decisions, and engage more fully with the present.

3. Emotional Health: Silence encourages emotional regulation. When we take time to relax and Improving reflect, we are better equipped to manage our emotions, leading to improved mental health and resilience. The practice of silence empowers us for approaching storms.

For silencing our monkey mind, consider the following practices:

1. Mindful Meditation: the ultimate practice for fostering silence and stillness. Activities and recordings in the daily plan guide you in mindful meditative practices. These practices quiet your thoughts and create a space for deeper insight.

2. Nature Walks: Spend time in nature, away from the distractions of urban life. The natural world provides a soothing backdrop for reflection and connection. Few things quiet the noise of life more naturally than the presence of a dog or a cat.

3. Journaling: Write down your thoughts, feelings, and desires in a journal. This practice can help you gain clarity about your needs and identify the true sources of nourishment in your life.

4. Digital Detox: Set aside specific times to unplug from technology. Doing so reduces mental clutter and creates space for deeper connections with yourself and others. When you strive to be your best self, it becomes easier to choose where to focus your mind.

Silencing the noise of daily life is an art one that helps you reconnect with your true self and desires. Give yourself the gift of stillness. Embrace quiet moments, and experience contentment and self-awakening. Be kind to your true self. Take heart: the path to self-discovery and authentic nourishment begins with embracing quiet serenity.

Fear

You will often hear that you should embrace your fear—that fear is a fundamental part of being human. Everyone experiences it, and it's okay to feel afraid. This is true in a normally functioning emotional system. Fear is healthy; it helps guide us through life's dangers. It is a critical part of the human survival mechanism, stimulating us to act in self-preservation. Embracing fear is as natural as being human fully aware and connected to oneself.

Imperfect fear, however, is not this healthy fear. It originates in a childhood where fear could not serve its intended purpose because it was constant and overwhelming. The child never feels safe and begins to fear not only external threats but the feeling of fear itself and the pain that comes with it. Every day and every night, the child lives in insecurity and dread. This type of fear cannot be embraced, as its persistent nature offers no resolution.

Understanding your fear isn't about what you fear; it's about why you fear. A person who experiences fear and panic in everyday situations is often dealing with these deeper, unresolved issues. They may fear flying, the dark, bridges, or even simply being outside around others. They may panic without an obvious trigger, even in ordinary moments. Layered onto this is the fear that these episodes might occur at an embarrassing time. They may dread others' judgment, worried that their fear reveals weakness or failure. Whatever the specific fear, addressing the underlying issues through a sensory-based approach can bring relief.

The instinctive response to fear is to fight or flee but what options did the child have? There was no escape. The only defense was to repress the emotion and minimize it as much as possible. Over time, this constant suppression every second of every minute, for weeks, months, and years became an ingrained defense mechanism. As a result, even healthy fear responses were shut down.

Healing doesn't come from dissecting the chronic fear of the past, but from allowing it to flow. According to the third law of emotion, when emotions are allowed to flow, all repressed feelings from childhood—including love, excitement, and joy—can flow with them. It doesn't matter whether imperfect fear stems from prolonged childhood circumstances or isolated traumatic events. The path to healing and restoring healthy fear is the same.

Play Beethoven on a coconut

If you want to play the beautiful music of your authentic self and express your uniqueness—your true nature of joy, happiness, and confidence—then you must have a great instrument to play that music. That instrument is your breath-body. In its natural state it's like a grand piano for playing the symphony of life. But when our breath-body instrument has been used to shut down our feelings, our music dies. When our childhood is too painful our breath-body freezes to minimize distress. Our breathing becomes small and irregular. Now when we want to play the music of our life, it's like playing Beethoven on a coconut.

Life is a symphony full of ups and downs. Sometimes you can feel stuck, like you're playing the same notes while everyone else is tackling a bigger, grander piece. So how do you get a chance to play something better? To be better? If you want to be all that you can be, then live a life where you choose joy and happiness with every breath. If you have the sense that you're not living your life to the fullest, you're not being all that you can be, then maybe your instrument isn't allowing you to play your true music—the you that you were designed to be; the full orchestra, the grand piano, all the violins, all the horns. What is needed is to liberate the instrument.

Playing a tense breathing instrument is frustrating and unrewarding. It's hard to find the rhythm, and mistakes are frequent. Tension chokes your feelings, shutting down your unique greatness with each and every breath. We shut down our emotions with our breathing, lowering our emotional IQ and making our lives difficult. Our feelings don't flow with our irregular breathing rhythm. And with breathing 24,000 times a day—8,000 times every night, we stay on defense, emotionally blocked.

Our breathing is imprinted with our childhood emotional feelings agitating those with every breath. As we breathe, we are subconsciously reminding ourselves what we can't have, what will never be. Why do we do this? Our involuntary breath-body is doing this and it will always control our thinking. The purpose was to survive childhood, but years later, the adult still suffers with the pain and fear of abandonment, neglect, abuse, and feeling invisible, unworthy, and unloved. The legacy of childhood has been passed onto the adult through the breathing instrument.

Normal pain and fear are a means to healing, a means to achieve what we desire. But the child's pain was constant, stemming from insecurity and fear. The tension in the breath-body was necessary and useful, but now, it is the worst kind of legacy. With every inhibited breath the adult suffers the sensations of early conditioning. The child's beautiful music was silenced, their pain and fear imprinted in the tension. Now the adult's great symphony of their life begs to be heard, but with such an instrument it's like trying to play Beethoven on a coconut.

Whatever we did in childhood was minimized. Now the question is: how do we maximize our great instrument to let our music play? How do we play the beautiful notes of life? How do we become in tune with our lives, harmonizing with those around us? We must liberate our breathing to free the music deep within. Stiff and tense, our breath-body will not harmonize. We must rid ourselves of the hard

Damage Childhood, Broken Relationships

As adults, individuals may struggle to form deep connections or accept love, often attracting partners who mirror unresolved childhood issues. Feelings of inadequacy and fear of abandonment can cloud emotional experiences, creating barriers to meaningful relationships. However, healing is possible and can be supported by embracing a richer, more sensory engagement with life. Opening up emotionally and allowing feelings to surface rather than keeping them repressed can be a transformative step.

One effective practice in this healing journey is breathwork. Through conscious deep breathing, individuals can begin to release physical tension and cultivate a deeper connection with themselves. While healing is a gradual process, each intentional breath and mindful moment contributes to the restoration of emotional well-being.

Adult Relationships after Childhood

As adults, many individuals find themselves struggling to form close relationships or accept love, often gravitating toward partners who reflect unresolved parental dynamics. Feelings of inadequacy and fear of abandonment can dominate their emotional landscape, making deep connection difficult. Yet, hope remains. The author suggests that healing is possible by engaging more fully with life through sensory experiences, encouraging readers to open up emotionally and release long-suppressed feelings.

Breathwork is emphasized as a vital practice in this process. Through conscious, deep breathing, individuals can begin to ease physical tension and foster a deeper sense of connection with themselves. Healing is not instantaneous, but with each intentional breath and mindful moment, one can gradually reclaim emotional well-being.

By embracing rather than avoiding life's experiences, individuals can move beyond repressed emotions and engage more richly with the world around them. It is essential to recognize that everyone holds the capacity to grow, heal, and rediscover joy. Although the path may feel overwhelming, every step toward shedding childhood defenses leads to a freer, more authentic life.

Remember: you are not alone in this process, and the potential for healing already resides within you. Embrace the journey.

Control is Repression and Avoidance

Maybe you're one of those people who are good at staying in control. It gives you pride and confidence. Some fear that if they lose control, they will be overwhelmed and unable to act thoughtfully. People often confess, "My emotions got the best of me," or "I couldn't help myself." The need for control actually stems from a fear of emotion. It was a way of numbing the inescapable pain and fear of a troubled childhood. Controlling the flow of emotions was the child's survival defense.

As adults, the strategy of repressing emotions to seek relief continues to dominate life strategies. Once it was a savior; now it governs one's entire life, creating emptiness within because repressing emotions is not selective, it's all or nothing. That's a high price to pay for control.

Humans often try to control themselves by stopping the flow of feelings and sensations. But this is ineffective it's like trying to dam a river. In truth, you can only redirect its flow and maybe minimize it. The river will still continue, just in unintended directions. It may spill over its banks, flooding forests and cities, destroying and damaging. It hasn't been controlled; it has been turned into a natural disaster. That's not control it's a colossal loss of it.

This is a defense against life itself: shutting it down, making it small. Every time fear, anger, or excitement arises, the response is the same control it. No real choice is made only a habitual reaction of closing down and tensing up to suppress true feelings. Surrendering choice to this reaction is the real loss of control.

Using control as the first and only response to stress makes you a slave to a childhood defense instead of a master of adult emotions. It's like locking yourself in a prison called "control" while convincing yourself it's for your own good. Not only do you become a slave to control, but you also shrink the flow of life's sensations. Life becomes smaller, less fulfilling. You are unable to feel its fullness.

You might say, "Well, that's the price I pay so I don't act crazily or wildly." I understand. In the past, when repressed anger erupted, it may have led to destructive behavior. That is scary. What once served a purpose in childhood is now making adult life much harder. But there is a better, more natural, and liberating way.

The control defense becomes unnecessary when you learn how to allow anger, excitement, fear and all emotions to flow as they were meant to. Real control is the freedom to respond with your full emotional range: fear, frustration, anger, excitement, respect. When feelings and sensations are allowed to flow, they don't stay the same they rise and dissolve according to their own weight and significance.

Controlling emotions is repression. Emotions are meant to rise and fall. Acceptance is true control. Denial through the need to control shuts everything down.

To live fully, the opposite of control is required: letting go. Allow all feelings and sensations to flow. This reveals your true self, making you visible for others to see and enjoy. Vulnerability, pain, excitement this is the human within you coming alive. Yes, anger and frustration may arise, but they won't explode. By letting go of the control defense, you reveal your unique, beautiful nature. This flow is true freedom. This is real control.

The principle of human technology at work here is that when we find stillness and quiet within ourselves letting go of ideas and overthinking—our emotions begin to flow as sensations. These sensations aren't labeled as anger or love, but experienced as life-enhancing physical feelings. Everything flows uninterrupted, uncensored. The river of sensation constantly changes. There are waterfalls, and deep calm pools. The river boils and then settles, narrows and widens. This is life. This is our life. Why try to control the impossible when we can enjoy the ride?

How to Live with Damaged Childhood

We think according to how we feel—this is our emotional baseline. If we're positive and optimistic, we tend to see life as full of opportunities. A gloomy and unhappy emotional baseline, however, can make us feel destined to struggle in all areas of life.

This emotional baseline is formed in childhood. That's fortunate if we had a nurturing upbringing, but less so if our childhood lacked essential support. The way we perceived ourselves as children shapes how we view life and our place within it.

The feelings and sensations we experience during our formative years—as babies, toddlers, and children lay the foundation for everything we build afterward. Our parents' outlook whether cheerful or grim, optimistic or pessimistic was either a gift or a burden. As a result, our present disposition, whether defensive or relaxed, angry or forgiving, stems directly from those early impressions. We didn't choose our level of contentment any more than we chose the circumstances of our birth.

Childhood experiences shape our lives not necessarily by what happened, but by how we felt about what happened. Even children within the same family can respond differently to similar situations. It's the emotional response that matters, not who was right or wrong, nor the degree of harm or trauma endured.

For a child, one need stands above all others. Whether a baby, toddler, or young child, there is one overriding concern—and it's the most powerful force in human nature: survival.

If a child, at any age, feels insecure or senses that their survival is threatened, they will instinctively develop strategies to strengthen their bond with their caregivers. It's not about being loved or loving it's about feeling safe.

And of course, this is exactly how the human species is designed. We don't emerge from the womb ready to run like a deer. We rely completely on our caregivers.

Enlightenment-how we function

Human technology

1. You are designed for success-handling all good/bad

2. Repression blocks you natural healing

3. You will heal as you are liberated. flowing is healing and thriving

4. Living is awareness of the stream of emotions, not thoughts

5. Focus

6. Impermanence of all

When you experience sensory and emotional flow, you are liberated. Within this flow is everything that you are not just the positive feelings you experience, but also the worries and fears. The nature of your human design is that all these emotions flow together, constantly moving one emotion blending with another, like balloons soaring high in the sky. Fear accompanies excitement. Anger coexists with courage and sadness. There is no "right" or "wrong," no "better" or "worse." All emotions carry equal weight, and all are valid. Repressing emotions and sensations throughout your life creates immense pressure. When you begin to release them, it can feel overwhelming at first. But stay calm and patient. The most intense emotions will fade and dissolve. This is true of your fears and worries, just as it is of your ecstasy and bliss. Nothing remains the same or gets stuck in the moment. You will learn that you can experience both great highs and deep lows while remaining relaxed and content.

Why why why?

Why? If we just know why, we can solve any problem we have, right? Why am I unable to find happiness? Why me? What is it that's made me so sad and depressed? Why do I do things I know are bad for me? Why can't we stop that behavior, that addiction, or that habit, when we finally realize it's controlling us? Why can't I be successful or have a loving relationship? I've solved so many problems by thinking about them; why can't I solve this? Why am I so miserable? Tell me why, please. I need to know why. Knowing why will set me free, and I'll do anything to find out. I'll read every book, talk to every therapist, and go to every retreat and treatment that promises me a better version of myself. I just need to know why?

"Why" is not a solution because the solution is not in the mind. It is in our body. Asking "why" keeps us trapped in a self-defeating, mentally exhausting loop. "Why" is like a rat's wheel, spinning and spinning with the appearance of progress but no forward movement. Thinking gives us the illusion of progress. It satisfies our big brains by assuming there's an answer waiting to be revealed to us with more insightful thinking. How do I find happiness? How do I find love? How do I discover my true purpose? So many therapies and self-help strategies center around thinking better as a solution to our problems. It's a mental maze with no exit. Our problems are human, not about physics or finance. We need to find humanistic answers. A computer cannot do this, not even the human one.

Answers are destined to fall short when searching for self-satisfaction. For one thing, answers are responses to questions, so they will never be better than the questions themselves. Answers are based on the choices we already have available to us. It's the questions that need resolution. In Buddhism, the questions of fear and pain are not answered by thinking. By letting go of ideas and focusing on seeing and feeling things as they are, answers arise from our deeper self. For liberation, let go of thinking.

We can go back in time to our childhood and discover many things, trying to make sense of it all. We try to understand how childhood led to where we are now, and maybe we do. But then we find that the more we know, the more questions arise. The greater our knowledge of "why" becomes, the more our ignorance is revealed (Kennedy and others).

The smarter we get, the better questions we ask. Yet each answer is like brushing away the sand from the stones of a buried pyramid. At first, you brush off enough sand until you find a flat, solid bottom. You think, "Now I really have something." Then you continue brushing, and the area expands, hard and solid. This must be what I'm looking for, you think. But then you find an edge, a corner, and you keep brushing. As you continue, you find there's another surface, another stone beneath. The more you brush, uncovering one stone after another, the more you realize it may take forever to reach the last stone. And then what? That last stone will be sitting on something much greater that will need exploration.

What we're truly trying to fix are the impulses that control our lives. These impulses and reactions are sensory and physical: impulses to avoid, to repress, to love, to use or drink, or to be angry and frustrated. The never-ending loop of thinking answers will not transform these. Our mind cannot fix itself any more than a sword can cut itself. Our impulses and responses are deeper than the mind. The answers or solutions to these impulses lie within our living selves, within those life sensations that flow from our deep, true self. This self is the one stone upon which all others sit.

Rational understanding may be valuable in relaxed situations, but under stress, the body is designed to overpower thinking. It will win every time. Get out of your mind, where most suffering lies. Let go of the need to know and grasp the meaning of it all. Stop telling the same stories while trying to explain yourself and what happened to you. Look within the body, which still holds the old pains and fears. Watch these and experience them now, in this moment. All we need to do is concentrate. In this way, we will experience knowing and healing ourselves. The questions of why will dissolve.Why?

"Why" is not a solution because the solution is not in the mind. It is in our body. Asking "why" keeps us trapped in a self-defeating, mentally exhausting loop. "Why" is like a rat's wheel, spinning and spinning with the appearance of progress but no forward movement. Thinking gives us the illusion of progress. It satisfies our big brains by assuming there's an answer waiting to be revealed to us with more insightful thinking. How do I find happiness? How do I find love? How do I discover my true purpose? So many therapies and self-help strategies center around thinking better as a solution to our problems. It's a mental maze with no exit. Our problems are human, not about physics or finance. We need to find humanistic answers. A computer cannot do this, not even the human one.

Answers are destined to fall short when searching for self-satisfaction. For one thing, answers are responses to questions, so they will never be better than the questions themselves. Answers are based on the choices we already have available to us. It's the questions that need resolution. In Buddhism, the questions of fear and pain are not answered by thinking. By letting go of ideas and focusing on seeing and feeling things as they are, answers arise from our deeper self. For liberation, let go of thinking.

We can go back in time to our childhood and discover many things, trying to make sense of it all. We try to understand how childhood led to where we are now, and maybe we do. But then we find that the more we know, the more questions arise. The greater our knowledge of "why" becomes, the more our ignorance is revealed (Kennedy and others).

The smarter we get, the better questions we ask. Yet each answer is like brushing away the sand from the stones of a buried pyramid. At first, you brush off enough sand until you find a flat, solid bottom. You think, "Now I really have something." Then you continue brushing, and the area expands, hard and solid. This must be what I'm looking for, you think. But then you find an edge, a corner, and you keep brushing. As you continue, you find there's another surface, another stone beneath. The more you brush, uncovering one stone after another, the more you realize it may take forever to reach the last stone. And then what? That last stone will be sitting on something much greater that will need exploration.

What we're truly trying to fix are the impulses that control our lives. These impulses and reactions are sensory and physical: impulses to avoid, to repress, to love, to use or drink, or to be angry and frustrated. The never-ending loop of thinking answers will not transform these. Our mind cannot fix itself any more than a sword can cut itself. Our impulses and responses are deeper than the mind. The answers or solutions to these impulses lie within our living selves, within those life sensations that flow from our deep, true self. This self is the one stone upon which all others sit.

Rational understanding may be valuable in relaxed situations, but under stress, the body is designed to overpower thinking. It will win every time. Get out of your mind, where most suffering lies. Let go of the need to know and grasp the meaning of it all. Stop telling the same stories while trying to explain yourself and what happened to you. Look within the body, which still holds the old pains and fears. Watch these and experience them now, in this moment. All we need to do is concentrate. In this way, we will experience knowing and healing ourselves. The questions of why will dissolve. Why?

"Why" is not a solution because the solution is not in the mind. It is in our body. Asking "why" keeps us trapped in a self-defeating, mentally exhausting loop. "Why" is like a rat's wheel, spinning and spinning with the appearance of progress but no forward movement. Thinking gives us the illusion of progress. It satisfies our big brains by assuming there's an answer waiting to be revealed to us with more insightful thinking. How do I find happiness? How do I find love? How do I discover my true purpose? So many therapies and self-help strategies center around thinking better as a solution to our problems. It's a mental maze with no exit. Our problems are human, not about physics or finance. We need to find humanistic answers. A computer cannot do this, not even the human one.

Answers are destined to fall short when searching for self-satisfaction. For one thing, answers are responses to questions, so they will never be better than the questions themselves. Answers are based on the choices we already have available to us. It's the questions that need resolution. In Buddhism, the questions of fear and pain are not answered by thinking. By letting go of ideas and focusing on seeing and feeling things as they are, answers arise from our deeper self. For liberation, let go of thinking.

We can go back in time to our childhood and discover many things, trying to make sense of it all. We try to understand how childhood led to where we are now, and maybe we do. But then we find that the more we know, the more questions arise. The greater our knowledge of "why" becomes, the more our ignorance is revealed (Kennedy and others).

The smarter we get, the better questions we ask. Yet each answer is like brushing away the sand from the stones of a buried pyramid. At first, you brush off enough sand until you find a flat, solid bottom. You think, "Now I really have something." Then you continue brushing, and the area expands, hard and solid. This must be what I'm looking for, you think. But then you find an edge, a corner, and you keep brushing. As you continue, you find there's another surface, another stone beneath. The more you brush, uncovering one stone after another, the more you realize it may take forever to reach the last stone. And then what? That last stone will be sitting on something much greater that will need exploration.

What we're truly trying to fix are the impulses that control our lives. These impulses and reactions are sensory and physical: impulses to avoid, to repress, to love, to use or drink, or to be angry and frustrated. The never-ending loop of thinking answers will not transform these. Our mind cannot fix itself any more than a sword can cut itself. Our impulses and responses are deeper than the mind. The answers or solutions to these impulses lie within our living selves, within those life sensations that flow from our deep, true self. This self is the one stone upon which all others sit.

Rational understanding may be valuable in relaxed situations, but under stress, the body is designed to overpower thinking. It will win every time. Get out of your mind, where most suffering lies. Let go of the need to know and grasp the meaning of it all. Stop telling the same stories while trying to explain yourself and what happened to you. Look within the body, which still holds the old pains and fears. Watch these and experience them now, in this moment. All we need to do is concentrate. In this way, we will experience knowing and healing ourselves. The questions of why will dissolve.

Need for Perfection

Perfectionists use perfection as a sword to slay the world around them, proving that, yes indeed, they know what is valuable, what is correct. if it's only in their ideal self-image and not in their deepest feelings. Striving for excellence can be motivating, but an obsession with perfection can be limiting. No action is completely perfect, and every decision has both positive and negative outcomes. Striving for perfection becomes its own obstacle when one cannot compromise to achieve results. The phrase "I'm a perfectionist" is often used to mask insecurities in an attempt to find self-worth where none exists.

Consider that when one proclaims themselves a perfectionist, they are creating a high standard which inevitably leads to failure. By doing this they maintain the undeserved and painful childhood feeling that they weren't loved or valued. So, in a perverse way, they compensate by creating failure by aiming for perfection, at work, in relationships, in the gym or in physical appearance. They may expect the same from others going so far to always be criticizing, mocking, or insulting. They assert superiority in intellect or talent. Some have the need to control people, habits, or every word they speak. It's exhausting and creates frustration and anger.

The problem is when errors and mistakes and inevitably arise and must be dealt with, ego has been crushed and they're unable to make creative adjustments. They give up altogether because deep down they don't believe any of it and feel they'll never get it right. That they themselves will never be right.

Errors show willingness to try and grow. Einstein made mistakes and was not afraid of pointing them out. Embrace mistakes as learning opportunities instead of letting perfectionism stop you from trying new things and feeling the satisfaction of learning. Base your actions on your desires and intentions rather than chasing perfection. Anytime you're chasing something you're not living now.

The entire world is imperfect, why should you be any different? There is decay. There are earthquakes and meteor showers. The whole cosmos is constantly dying and being reborn. Your choice to engage with R/T reflects your desire for self-improvement and initiative-taking action. Align perfection with your highest intentions and best efforts then let successes and failures occur where they will. When you make a mistake don't turn it into a statement about who you are. It's something you did. The best anyone can do, the closest to perfection we can come, is when we act with self-respect and honor. Give yourself room to breathe and be the beautiful, imperfect creature you are.

Letting go

Just let go, people say, that's all you have got to do. Letting go is a popular idea. If I let go, will I be free. Freedom sounds good. Free to be my best self. Free of my demons, my habits and self-destructive behavior. How do I let go? What do I let go of to be free? Thoughts? Yes, thoughts and ideas that are obstructing happiness and fulfillment. But all I know are thoughts. If I am what I think, who will I be If I let go of my thoughts?

We want to be free from our thoughts so we can let go of all the disturbing worries and memories. After all, 99% of our thoughts are not really ours. We didn't originate them. They came in to us through our environment, our culture, our friends, our social network Yes they're in our mind so we believe we own them. But those 99% thoughts would be completely different if we had lived in a different time in a different place with different family and friends. Maybe we have 1% of original creative or intuitive thoughts or ideas of our own. even for thoughts about who we are. Our very identity would change because all these thoughts have been given to us.

Could it be possible that we're not who we think we are? It is said we believe 100% of what we tell ourselves, 50% of what we hear and 10% of what we read. And they are all our thoughts. But what are we telling ourselfves? If we let go of all of our thoughts, what remains? Buddhists say that our true essence is awareness, love, and compassion, and that these are outside of our thinking. You mean I'm not an angry uptight pessimistic human? No, all of those things we're given to you by your circumstances. Along with the ideas I'm a bodybuilder, I'm a businessman, I'm a housewife, I'm a husband, I'm a father, I'm an achiever. Along with I'm no good, I'm not worthy, I'm not lovable, I'm a sad person. Whatever we do, all come from our conditioned thinking.

So, you say well that's all fine, but I can't change my circumstances. No, but yes you can let go of your absolute belief in your ideas. The method for achieving release involves consistent practice of mindful and serene living. This is facilitated through the activities outlined in the daily plan. By engaging in mindful and tranquil practices, a gap is created between conditioned thoughts and one's true nature. True nature emerges as an experience from the deep, quiet place within. Through these practices, individuals can relinquish all harmful thought patterns. Consequently, we encounter our true, profound nature—our inherent self—that remains unaffected by external circumstances or our own thought processes.

Let us go to where words don't reach; where concepts fall away; where mind drops. It is not an empty void; it is not a pessimistic nothingness. We've been influenced our whole life to look at the world through a colored lens in which everything is distorted. How can we see things as they are in the world? How can we see our own lives with clarity? How can we see our problems, our suffering, even our happiness though these false lenses? We cannot because we have always learned about the world through this filter. It is all we know.

Truly, all we have to do is to let go. When we let go, when, for the first time, we put down our false view, everything is there! All things self-manifest, naturally, as they are, without any coloration, without our lens or anyone else's. It is we who are absent. It's just this! Does the world disappear? No, it is there. In fact, everything becomes pristine clear, as opposed to being cloudy and confused. It was confusing because everything was about having and not having, good and bad, success and failure, yes and no. Once all drops away, we actually see things as they are. Then the full potential of everything happens in its own harmony.

Dreaming and Envisioning

When was the last time you imagined your best life? Imagined doing the things that you most enjoy, being with the people that make you happy, and living with purpose and satisfaction? Many people think about their best life but don't know how to imagine it. And imagining is such a great power that it brings us face to face with those things we want most. It drives us towards those things we want the most. It's a powerful motivation.

Many people dream of the past in such a way that it's real to them. They feel it, relive it, suffer the same sadness, or enjoy the great moments again. But they don't do the same for their future. They don't envision it specifically and with such detail that they can experience the joy of what they desire before they achieve it. Why not? If we can go back to connect with past experience, our pain, disappointments, and triumphs, why don't we use the same power to grasp our happy future?

Envisioning is a skill. It's sometimes known as manifesting. Here are a couple of tips for improving it. First, shut your eyes and imagine all the situations that will come with receiving your desires. Imagine yourself living a life of contentment and satisfaction. Imagine people around you enjoying this with you. You find yourself smiling and content. Enjoy these scenes in your head the same as you might remember past experiences. Never mind it hasn't happened yet. Immerse yourself in it. See, taste, smell, touch the visions in your head. Find reasons to laugh and enjoy them. Practice often to refine new skill.

Secondly, allow your imaginary feelings to penetrate deeply within your body. Breathe and accept them to become a part of your body, not remain cold visions in your mind. Connect with the feelings of peace and well-being from living that life. When your desires become so real to you that you don't know where reality stops and imagination starts, then you're living them now. The fruits will start falling all around you.

Emptiness.

Emptiness and a hollow feeling can only be filled by connecting and experiencing your true self. Why can't I fill the void? Maybe, you're trying to fill void with the self you constructed not your true self. You're filling it up with decisions and choices based on fear and pain from the past. You're seeking to be justified, approved. And acknowledged by people and situations long ago. You are all about more achievements and your possessions. You define yourself by what you have or what you don't have. Where is the inner truth?

Who is your true self? You were cut off from experiencing your true self before you were old enough to know what self is by repressive defenses to pain and fear. Not your fault. You were brain-washed by neglect and manipulation beginning at a time before memory. All this conditioning filled your mind until your 40,000 thoughts a day are now controlling and defining you. Is there any wonder you don't know who you truly are or what's your purpose in life? You are playing a game handed to you. The rules were rooted in you like the rules of chess tattooed on your forehead. You're moving the pieces but this is not your game. You are a slave to this fabricated self, installed upon an empty mind. It's no surprise you feel empty. The void is not you. It is in your mindless thinking, your precious ideas.

The daily mindful practices and activities connect you to your body and to the knowledge of true you. Concentrate upon your body giving yourself space and quiet from your thinking self. You will discover increasing fullness that comes from this experience. Satisfaction with life will arise. Choose to stop thinking for one minute and breathe. Your thoughts have betrayed you and constructed this emptiness. Why listen to them when there's so much more of you? Breathe to know you are breathing. Choose yourself over the shadow self of your mind.

Understanding Emotional Healing

Everything that happened to us as children first came to us through sensations. Later came thought and ideas. Therefore, isn't it ludicrous to think that we're going to modify and heal those hurtful childhood sensations with an idea?

It is crucial to recognize that the experiences and feelings we encounter in childhood often manifest through sensations rather than abstract thoughts. The events that affect a child deeply resonate within their sensory perceptions—these experiences create lasting impressions that can shape their emotional well-being. Considering this, it seems somewhat unreasonable to believe that we can address and heal these profound sensations solely through intellectual concepts or ideas.

To effectively navigate the path toward healing, we must first acknowledge the significance of these sensations. Instead of relying solely on thoughts to process our experiences, it is essential to engage with our feelings on a deeper, more sensory level. This approach encourages us to cultivate awareness of our sensations, leading to a better understanding of our emotional responses.

By fostering this awareness and allowing ourselves to connect with our true feelings, we can embark on a journey of healing that embraces our entire being. We are encouraged to explore various methods—such as mindfulness, body awareness, or creative expression—that can help us process these sensations in a meaningful way. This is not only an empowering path toward healing but also a vital step in nurturing our emotional resilience. Embrace this journey, and remember that true healing often comes from within, guided by our innate sensory experiences.

Not your fault

Unhappiness and discontent are not inherent qualities. Individuals attempting to overcome ineffective coping mechanisms developed in childhood should understand that it is the coping methods that are flawed, not themselves. The environment and conditions in which one was raised play a significant role in shaping stress management strategies.

Childhood experiences provide us with our perspective on life and our basic emotional state. A child could only do as much as they were permitted and supported to do. Therefore, adults who experienced demeaning and stressful childhood conditions often face difficulties later in life.

The child was not broken; rather, its healthy coping systems and thriving attitude were compromised from infancy through childhood. As the child grows into adulthood, they carry this compromised operating system and strive to manage as best they can. It is not a lack of effort or capability on the part of the adult.

The root cause lies in the disrupted development during childhood, not in the adult. Just as it was not the child's fault for being born into adverse circumstances, it is not the adult's fault either. Low self-esteem in adults may stem from early childhood imprinting.

By engaging in mindful practices and addressing the issues that originated in childhood, adults can renew themselves. With dedication, self-esteem, self-love, and confidence can be restored, as the core operating system remains intact.

Hanging on to the Past

Memory serves as a way to attempt to capture and retain our experiences, but it only provides an impression of past events rather than concrete answers.

Instead, using a method of focus can be more effective. By concentrating on feelings and sensations, one can find deeper insights. Focusing on your breath and body may lead to answers within yourself.

Often, memory can be clouded by emotions or altered by time, making it unreliable for finding absolute truths about our past. In contrast, grounding oneself in the present moment through practices like mindfulness or meditation can calm the mind and enhance clarity. For instance, paying attention to the rhythm of your breath can help you connect with your inner thoughts and emotions, providing a pathway to self-discovery.

Moreover, focusing techniques such as progressive muscle relaxation or guided imagery can help relieve stress and promote mental well-being. Engaging in these practices consistently might reveal patterns or solutions that were not apparent when relying solely on fragmented memories.

Incorporating regular mindfulness exercises into your routine can also strengthen your ability to remain present and attentive in daily life. This heightened state of awareness can improve decision-making, boost emotional regulation, and foster a greater understanding of oneself and others.

By embracing the present and tuning into physical and emotional cues, you can unlock deeper layers of insight that are often obscured by the fleeting nature of memory. This approach not only enriches personal growth but also enhances overall mental health and resilience.

Knowing yourself

Who am I? What should I be doing in life? How do I know myself? Buddhists teach about two selves within us: the conditioned self and the true self, sometimes referred to as monkey mind and true mind. If it's difficult to grasp but there is two of us in a very real sense it's because we're trying to grasp it with one self, the thinking self. The true self we don't find by thinking. We may call it the true mind but it's really a consciousness of being present. To know this self is only possible through quiet and calm experiencing, which is done with the guided activities in this program.

It is within this true original self where we find higher consciousness and intuitive sense of well-being. If you wanna know what it looks like watch toddler or a young child who feels secure and trusting, they are at one with the world around them and nothing can happen for them to lose that sense of the true self. They are full of love and excitement and curiosity this is our true original self and it's within each and every one of us no matter the severity of our conditioning and training to destroy our self-love and well-being. When we create space from our busy monkey mind quiet focused practice, we can see that that is not us but who is observing that mind, those thoughts? Here's our original authentic self. The self of empowerment. The original self, the un-erasable, undeletable self.

The Conditioned Self

The conditioned self consists of everything you have ever seen, sensed, or been told. You have been conditioned or trained into this life. Initially, your conditioned self was empty. However, you were not empty; you had an original self, the true self. All of our problems reside in the conditioned self, influencing how we think and feel about life. It's our life view.

The True Self

Your true essence and the meaning of your life are found in your true self—the self that came installed. All of your training and conditioning were added on top of that original self. If the training and conditioning align with that original self, you will feel peaceful and contented. If the training and conditioning you received were not harmonious with your original self, you will feel empty, discontented, and hollow. This true self will arise and become the dominant self in our life when we release all the layers and imprinting from our conditioning.

Recognizing the True Self

So, how do we recognize our original self if we accept everything we've been told, seen, and heard as ourselves? When we seek to understand ourselves, which self are we referring to? Naturally, we aim to discover our original, authentic self. Exploring the conditioned, trained mind provides little insight into our true nature.

Small, smaller, smallest

From our inborn desire to please our parents and seek their love, we subconsciously cut off our emotional expression to avoid rebuke. We make ourselves less of a target by becoming smaller and smaller, even to the point of shallow breathing. We are conditioned to get small and quiet, to avoid drawing negative attention to ourselves, and to make ourselves more desirable to our parents. Many children learn early on that emotional expressions evoke punishment from parental figures. From not being picked up are comforted while crying to hearing [phrases like "be quiet," "don't make noise," or "just be a good boy or girl" reverberate in memory. These shaped our responses and behavior and continue in adult behaviors like being a people pleaser and using childhood strategies for seeking attention and love.

Getting small leads to nervous impulses, and embedded breath and body tension. Due to the child's lack of comfort and nurturing of emotional expression, adults often say, "I'm fine," while internally desiring connection and affirmation. The need for love and affirmation was never learned or allowed to be expressed. It's crucial to recognize that this desire for love and acceptance is universal. It's the damaged child's strategies for obtaining it that creates discontentment and anguish. Breathe big, be big to ask and expect the love you want.

5

How To's for Living Life

The basic skills for living life are the same as the five horsemen. We need to learn how to apply them to every situation. It may require letting go of some of our conditioned ideas, and, in some cases, facing our fears. Life gets simpler as we practice more of these skills and become more adept at using them in our life. Life is not meant to be a struggle and you are not meant to struggle. You will see a theme and these instructions on living well. Though there may be specific methods and techniques, the theme is as old as man himself because it's how are human technology functions. Buddhists have built one of the greatest healing practice and instructions over the last 2600 years based upon this technology. Apply these techniques and you will notice life becoming easier, richer, and more satisfying.

How to breathe for liberation.

1. Stick your stomach out as if you had swallowed a football and leave it relaxed out even as you exhale.
2. Breathe deeply into this stomach area
3. Once the stomach fills let the chest rise until you can feel ribs moving all the way around to your spine.
4. When the chest is filled allow the diaphragm to stretch.
5. Exhale without effort.

Many people have tension like a Python wrapped tightly around their chest and stomach, preventing natural breathing under stressful conditions. Natural breathing, full and fluid, is how we process our emotions and stress. Abnormal tension squeezing the chest and stomach was created by relentless stress, most likely in childhood. It is unnatural, but it is normal for many. This stressful breathing puts their emotional state I'm an autopilot set to fear and trauma. With this breathing technique we stretch and liberate the python's grip upon us restoring our natural system. As our system is restored to its natural state so is our original emotional state. The state of love and compassion within each and every one of us.

We breathe somewhere around 22,000 times a day. If your breathing instrument is not able to function to its highest capacity and in a fluid manner, then it's not operating the way it was designed. All our fears and worries become ingrained with our breathing. By creating a more physically free breathing instrument we immediately improve our emotional state, becoming more positive, more confident, more relaxed, and more clear headed. By practicing conscious breathing procedures designed to liberate our instrument, we reset this automatic pilot to our original state of loving, compassionate, and aware.

How to strengthen focus.

To focus for strength. 1 pick a sensory object like your breath flowing in and out, a sound of a bell or a ticking clock, or the movement of your stomach rising and falling t. Two. Consciously focus upon the object. 3 if you become aware of any conceptual thoughts, ideas, or feelings and sensations interrupting your focus, come back to the object, letting the distractions go on without you. 4. practice this daily until you can do it for 5 minutes, then 10 then 15 and so on.

Few realize that you can strengthen your focus. And if you can strengthen your focus then you don't get lost in every thought and every problem. Every time you come back to the object, you will increase your strength of focus and you will be able to remain focused upon the object with less effort. By maintaining focus for longer periods of time you increase your awareness and mental strength. When an emotional storm or a chaotic moment comes, you will remain calm and clear and know exactly what and if anything needs to be done. Focus is a fundamental strength for living a great life.

How to quiet your thoughts.

You are not the only one to ask this question, how do I stop thinking? Many people want to quiet their mind. Many are worn out by their endless thinking. Our upsetting thoughts spinning around our heads without any control or censor. It is said that we have 40,000 thoughts a day. How can anyone cope with this endless stream of distraction? People want to get out of their head and to finally have some peace and calm. Night and day, day and night thinking, thinking, thinking. It can be exhausting.

How do we stop it? We try everything to distract ourselves from our thoughts. Normal activities we transform into addictions to escape our mental selves; cleaning, talking, eating and drinking, and working. We go to movies, go shopping, we talk endlessly on the phone, and, of course, scroll through all our social media. We will do literally anything to get away from the constant stream of thoughts. We occupy ourselves with superficial and meaningless behaviors. City people say they love the city-life; relentlessly stimulating with a barrage of sounds, smells, and friction of all kinds human and mechanical. They can't walk around the corner without changing their direction or their pace every six steps. Their attention is to busy living. It keeps them engaged with life but not engaged in themselves..

Would it shock you to know we can actually think better if we know how to quiet our mind? But quieting our mind is not the right way to think about it. You are never going to stop the 40,000 thoughts. The most remote monk on the highest mountain meditating for the longest time in history did not stop his thoughts. True he gave himself space and stillness on the mountaintop but that's not how he quieted his mind. He actually let his thoughts go. He let his thoughts continue without him so to speak.

How does he do this? Can we escape our thoughts like a monk? Yes, it's called being. But not merely being, it's being on a very profound level, It's an inner space where you become more aware of everything in your life. The flow of sensations and feelings within and from without are more intense, richer. You become tuned in to your personal music, the deep essence of yourself. All of this occurs naturally when we quiet the mind by being more present in the moment. This is the open secret of the monk.

This is a skill unlike any other skill. It's a natural skill, mostly underdeveloped, which you can greatly improve to quiet the mind. It's based upon the human technology principle of maintaining awareness. When a human maintains awareness for longer periods of time, they drop out of their thinking mind into the pure state of being. In this state there is no attachment to concepts or ideas. The spinning thoughts are left as they are without any attention or concern for them. This is what the monk does.

This is explaining something that there are no words. It's an experience, an experience within your reach by following the activities in this guide. I like the analogy of the quiet us being a clear blue sky. The clouds in the sky are our thoughts. There are bright white clouds, there are dark ominous clouds, there are storms big and sometimes devastating. Above all is the constancy of our being the clear blue sky. The sky never changes, only the clouds under it are always changing. Clouds come, they go, they rise and fall with the cycle of life. When we are aware of our true nature as being the clear blue sky, and not the clouds of thinking, we will not follow or be disturbed by movements of the storms and clouds. This requires a strong and frequent practice of focus and awareness. Skills which will be developed while following the activities in this guide.

How to let go of all life-numbing tension.

1. Focus your mind's eye upon a sensory object. You could focus upon a sound, smell, taste, or touch. Or focus upon physical movement like one does in yoga. The walking sensations from the bottom of your feet pressing down on the ground with each step is a great sensory object for releasing tension. All of these focus techniques require maintaining focus for longer periods, not fleeting focus. All ideas or thoughts are distracting and interfere with releasing tension. The more often you do this, the better you feel.

2. Focus upon your breath/breathing. There are many techniques for using breath focus. I've given you a few in this guide and in the

recording links. The principle is the same: not merely focusing but maintaining for 5/10/30 minutes or more.

3. There are many good and great techniques for releasing tension but not as good as a skilled focusing practice. Body surveys are where you start with your toes and with your mind's eye identifying and releasing tension as you move your way up and around your body. Tensing and relaxing a body part, like your fists, for one to four minutes can be effective. Try as many as you can.

If all you do is to release tension 24 hours a day, seven days a week your life will never be the same. Tension is a killer of life, of your life spirit. No psychological therapies, no new logical thinking, and no new ideas come anywhere close to transforming your life as does releasing tension. Tension In your body restricts your life channels where your river of sensations flow. If your sensory flow is restricted you're not connected to your life. You're not connected to each moment of life fully. And if you're not connected you're don't have the information, the awareness to make good decisions or to get more pleasure out of life.

In Eastern teachings these channels are sometimes referred to as chakras. It is generally agreed that your life energy, all your sensations, flow through your root chakra. This is located deep in your belly. Is it any wonder that children with stressful family lives complain of stomach pain? Or that as adults we have many gut-wrenching issues and problems? Modern somatic therapies focus on this area. When we do conscious relaxation of tension we are merely relaxing our shell that which we have song voluntary control. But it's this visceral tension, subconscious and deeply embedded within us, which can be affected only by voluntarily focusing away from our thinking and into our bodies. And this is where life-numbing tension needs to be released for long lasting transformation.

How to chant.

1. Hear the sound precisely as it comes out of your mouth.
2. Notice the vibrations and follow them all the way into your belly.
3. Relax. If you lose your way, simply come back to the chant.

Chatting is a great method for getting out of your head. My close friend and first Zen teacher always used to say, it's like a laser. I couldn't understand what she meant for many years although I enjoyed it and felt better afterwards. Then one day it became clear to me. Like a sharp laser it cleans out all your thoughts from your busy mind leaving you with clarity and calm.

The method uses the sound of the word syllables as the object of your focus. Zen tradition uses a rhythm beat on a wooden drum (Mokugyo) which we coordinate the phonetic translation of the Japanese. The chant in the recording I've given you is from the heart sutra. It loosely means, among various translations, I've gone, gone to the other side to enlightenment. Just read the chant and follow the beat. After a short while you won't need to read and you can keep you own beat if you wish. You will experience the laser effect.

How to comfort nervous system with vibration.

1. Take a deep breath and say the word, Mu, until the sound/vibration fades. Repeat 5 times.
2. Take a deep breath and say the word, Vu, until the sound/vibration fades. Repeat 4 times.
3. Same as before but using the word, Ah. Repeat 3 times.

Ask yourself which one of these sounds, Mu, Vu, Ah, had the most intense vibration/sensation? Exactly where in your body is the center of each sound?

This process connects the vibrations in your body with your consciousness. 2. Operates on your nervous system to comfort anxiety and open your sensory flow.

Eastern practices have been using the word MU (emptiness or nothingness) for centuries. Vu is a word used by the somatic innovator, Levine. But you don't have to know anything About them or your nervous system for it to have an effect upon you. Just do it to comfort yourself period to give yourself a little peace. It's something you see children do reflexively. Add it to your nighttime routine or anytime you need a little peace and comfort.

How to eat less for more flavor.

1. Look at the food in front of you the colors, the textures. Try to smell without moving your nose each of the different foods. Now look around you holding those sights and smells in your experience.

2. Pick up the utensil slowly. Feel the weight in your hand. Which finger is more sensitive? Notice the temperature changes on your fingertips. You may see light or reflection if it's a metal utensil. If it's chopsticks, you'll notice the texture of the wood or finish.

3. Pick up the selected food and as you move it towards your mouth, look at it seeing the details of this particular bite and how it sits upon the utensil.

4. Put The food in your mouth. Lay down the utensil before you start chewing. Then chew the food as you calmly look around you. Chew it two or three times longer than you normally do noticing how the flavors move and change.

5. If you must speak wait until you swallow. Do not speak with food in your mouth or utensil in your hand.

6. Begin again.

This may seem very awkward but it's just eating consciously. It is probably a lot slower than you normally eat. But what is the proper amount of time to eat? Make this a habit and it will begin to flow easily without much thought. You will find that mealtimes will become much more enjoyable. You will eat for pleasure and nourishment instead of mindlessly comforting anxieties with large quantities of uninteresting food.

Eating, or anything we do, will be more interesting if we do so mindfully. More flavor, more texture, more enjoyment of the food we're eating when we eat consciously. We will eat less with more satisfaction. It's as if our taste buds have suddenly awakened to new dimensions of food. Maintaining your mindfully connected lifestyle throughout the day gives more inner peace and contentment and eating is the perfect way to maintain that connection.

How to create purpose.

1. Sit in a quiet place.
2. Focus upon your stomach rising and falling with your breath.
3. When your mind wanders and you're distracted, return your focus to your stomach.

This is a frequent question, what is my true purpose in life? It seems if we know our true purpose in life, we will be happy and successful, doesn't it? What does this procedure have to do with it? How can sitting and watching your breathing have anything to do with ones purpose?

When a person practices being quiet and still, so quiet that that thinking and ideas fade into the background, an amazing experience takes place. A deep peace and contentment arise. This sets free a profound sense of oneself, unlike any previously experienced. Contact with ones true self is made. For many it is like meeting a stranger from another planet.

This only happens when long-conditioned and habitual thinking no longer exerts power over one's self-beliefs. It's only with practicing quiet and profound stillness that one finds deep, true self.

A person begins to sense their true nature after freeing themselves from the habits and thought training since childhood. This liberation is critical to overcome persistent childhood stress. The quiet practices described here are effective and necessary to free oneself from this conditioning. Once liberated from these erroneous notions of self, our genuine purpose becomes clear. Conflicting purposes between practical considerations and the deeper self can result in a sense of emptiness, as practicality often does not fulfill deeper needs, and may hinder the discovery of one's true purpose in life.

How to let yourself flow.

Flow is our natural way of healing. Flow is our natural way of living. Tension is the gate keeper of flow. Releasing tension from our breath-body will allow flow, because physical tension blocks free and healthy flow. Bodily tension represses our exuberance and our optimism for living. Tension shuts down creativity in our natural intuitiveness. Tension makes us and our lives small by persistently agitating our emotional stress. It's as if we have an electrical current buzzing through us night and day.

Creating and liberating flow is not a mental process but a physical one. It is through the physical body, particularly our breathing instrument, that we open our sensory and emotional flow. Any tension in our body restricts flow. Buddhists teach that tension obstructs our life channels. These channels where our sensations and feelings from living pass. These tension blocks can be found anywhere, our throat, in our belly, in our back. They are all related to our stress. Removing one block helps to release another one and reduce emotional stress. As we create more flow, we feel better.

Why would a critical, natural process like sensory flow become blocked? This is our childhood's defense against pain and fear and other overwhelming childhood emotions. Repressing sensations and feelings is the ultimate survival strategy of dysfunctional childhood. Although it's a childhood strategy, this damaged defense system continues into adulthood. It is the only strategy and all ideas are constructed on top of it. The adult will never be happy until the natural strategy of allowing sensory flow is learned.

Flow is what naturally happens when your mind and body are free. By human design, the sensations of life flow through us. The sensations of touch, sight, taste, touch and sound are the five acknowledged ways we experience life, though there are many others. Sensations from these are constantly flowing through us keeping us calm and feeling connected. Notice that all sensations and feelings we receive through our body. But when this flow is blocked or repressed, we become very unhappy and emotionally unstable. We are then disconnected from our bodies, making our lives seem meaningless and empty.

By ignoring our sensory flow or self-distracting, we are not aware of life's vibrancy all around us. We are not tuned in and awake. Buddhists teach if not connected to these bodily sensations we're not living fully in the present moment. When we're occupied with mental tasks from work or social media, we become sensorily and emotionally disconnected from our bodies. We distract ourselves with our habits and addictions trying to avoid the pain and fear our we never processed in childhood. On the other hand, letting ourselves flow heals us and gives us to have a richer life.

Instead of anger becoming rage and overwhelming us, it flows and dissolves. Instead of grief lingering and consuming our lives, it lessens its grip. Sadness rises and falls without depression. Joy and bliss, too, rise into the vapor, leaving contentment and satisfaction. This is the natural design of our flowing emotions and sensations, keeping us healthy and happy, never repressed or trapped in an emotion, never creating obstacles of gloom within us.

You'll experience this yourself by following the activities in this guide. There are activities and exercises for releasing tension. There are procedures for focusing on your breath-body thereby connecting you to your flow. As you practice these things you're learning, and the longer and more frequent your practice, the more flow you will create. Because you don't work on flow directly. You become quieter and still, connecting to your non-thinking self. As flow is restored your life becomes fuller.

How to manage anger.

There are two kinds of justifiable anger. The first is justifiable because people are hurting people, governments are oppressing people, children are in pain. These are justifiable objects of anger. But these don't have to be managed. The anger justifiably rises within us encouraging us to do something, to help someone. This is healthy, compassionate anger. It doesn't require management. It comes from our decency and our morality and only asks from us positive action. It has its own weight and presence. It's not to be avoided but acknowledged.

The other kind of justifiable anger is the anger which consumes us. We seek personal justification in our anger so as not to appear crazy or evil. When we blow up, enraged at another driver, retail clerk, or at our spouses or children, we need justification to mask our own embarrassment and sense of defeat. It can't be our fault, we justifiably think, because *they* are making us angry, *they're* causing our rage. Eventually we exhaust our justifications. We can't formulate a new one that we believe. We see over and over the innocence of the many objects of our rage. Deep down we begin to glimpse ourselves and our phony justifications. We cannot hide anymore. That's if we are lucky. Sometimes there needs to be a catastrophic revelation before we understand that there is no justification on earth big enough to match our rage. This is the anger which needs to be managed. First, we need to observe it.

Justification shields us from looking within ourselves and changing. If we are right and they are wrong, then our self-destructive anger is okay. Why do we do this? It feels like we have no control. This unmanageable anger is coming from childhood where life defenses developed against fear and pain. Now, we seek revenge. In childhood we repressed our anger, now, we want to let our anger out. All the anger bottled up in our child, due to treated as invisible, unlovable, can now be vented. We were always accused without reason. It was always our fault but we didn't know why. The anger built within us until we were ten, eleven, twelve and had a little room to vent. We were mad as hell and not going to take it anymore. From then on we're going to give it back to the world as often as we can in any way that we could. We would get revenge every day for the rest of our lives. And if we couldn't find someone to vent to we would turn it on ourselves.

There is justification for this overwhelming, self-eating anger but it's not in any presumed insults in our present life. The justification is in the pain of the child within. The child lived a torturous childhood filled with painful thoughts and fear. If I can't be loved, then nobody should be loved. I'm not going to love them because they won't love me. My mission now is to destroy, to belittle, and to frighten. I'll get avenge all the things done to me ten times over. I don't care what happens to me. Why should I care, nobody else does. I will burn down every relationship until I get my due. The world is against me, I know, but I will show the world true pain with my rage. I will storm against anyone who tries to get close because I know it's all a lie, and, by God, that makes me angry.

So, this damaged child is now an adult. Maybe you were that child and are struggling to manage your anger. Maybe now you can see that your anger is coming from a justifiable place. The child you were deserves to be angry. But now your anger is not going to satisfy that long ago injustice. Your actions now aren't justifiable even as the child's anger is. They deserve their anger, but why should you beat yourself now with such self-destructive emotion? Why extend his pain by hurting as many people as you can? Do you really need to prove to the world how hurtful your childhood was? Who in the world are you trying to prove it to anyway?

Open up, let your anger flow. You can heal your anger now in ways your child never could. Your child was trapped. If they healed their anger causing pain, they were hit immediately with new pain. They were living the pain and the fear and the anger every second of every day, every week, and every month for years. There was no escape. It's like being continually cut. Healing is impossible. This is not your situation. You are free to reason or walk away. There's no basis in your present reality to stay angry. As you resolve your anger you can change your situation.

You may be saying to yourself now your anger is bigger than you. That's because you have never really looked at it as an adult. It was bigger than your child and you've been living with that perception all these years. The truth is if you really watch your anger, allow the sensations of your anger to flow, you will not be overwhelmed. It's like watching a storm. The wind blows, lightning crashes, and the storm fades away. The sun appears. But you've never done that because your child wasn't able to do it. You are able and you can. And you will see the storm rise and fall.

With all emotions like anger think of them as the sensations they are. Watch the sensory-emotion you call anger. These impulses and feelings in your body your mind calls anger. But they are much more than that. When you feel these impulses in your body count to two or three before you make any movement.

Give yourself a little space between the impulse and your action. When you do this you will connect sometimes to what you experienced in childhood. More importantly, you will notice you don't have to react in the habitual way. The more space you give between the impulse and the action the more choices you have and how to act and what to do. You may even find you don't have to feel angry anymore. You may find that interesting. By watching your sensations, you have more power to manage what you call anger. You might find that it is essentially a continuous flow of sensations rising and falling, changing and dissolving.

How to see reality

Buddhists say what we call reality is an illusion, that none of it is reality. What we call reality is constructed in our minds. Could this be true and if it is then what is reality? And what does it matter anyway because all we have is our minds. We have no other way of seeing reality but through our mind and our sensory perceptions. It all seems very philosophical with not much practical application. But Buddhists also say that all of our problems are from our thoughts and our busy minds. And if this is true reality becomes a huge issue because what Buddhists are saying is that our perception of reality that's causing all our problems and preventing our contentment and satisfaction.

Let's look at how we can actually do something about the reality we tell ourselves and the reality we're seeking for our happiness and success. First we have to accept that everything in our mind was not there when we were born. We have been trained and conditioned by our upbringing in our circumstances to think a certain way and to have a certain philosophy and life strategies. We weren't born with any of this. And if we were born 100 years or 1000 years ago or 100 years in the future to a different family or different culture we wouldn't have the same view of life. Our reality would be vastly different. The way we looked at relationships and family and work and pleasure would be different. We would view the reality of the world differently. But are we hopelessly trapped in our minds or can we be the masters of it? Can we change reality?

So, if everything in the mind is a false reality and an illusion what is the alternative? The alternative is very simple. When we focus upon our sensory flow we create space from our thinking mind and what is often called higher consciousness. This is a consciousness of non-think, no thoughts or concepts. Yes, it is possible through this natural process of focusing upon an object like breathing, or a candle, or any object whatsoever, we can escape the trap of our incessantly spinning thoughts. This higher consciousness reveals to us a new reality about ourselves and our world.

Focusing upon an object creates higher consciousness? This seems way too simple for something so profound. But it is the basic process to free us from the illusions of reality that we've been conditioned. And as we free ourselves from false reality, guess what? We become free from our problems, our disturbances, our issues. Free from all of the ideas we have in our head, what is left? Who are we? What do we think about life and what is the reality we're living? The only way to know is to experience this higher consciousness by the practice of focusing and put in effort upon an object as we do in these daily program activities.

What we will find is we don't need labels and explanations of ourselves or our lives. We don't need to judge everything for quality or correctness. We are released from the obligation of self-criticism. All of the tension and all of the weight of this lifetime of mental training and being a slave to our minds dissolves. And what emerges is our true nature. What is this true nature that contains our purpose and meaning of life? Well, you can see it in any child two years old who feels safe and secure. The essence of our true nature as love, self- love and compassion for ourselves and for others. In this total and complete love there is no fear, no obstacles. This is our true nature, which some Buddhists call the true self the true mind. Imagine a life built upon this instead of all the thoughts and concepts we've been told and were indoctrinated with from babyhood through childhood.

How to Build Confidence

Confidence comes not from bravado but from self-esteem. We build self-esteem by taking action that is in harmony with our true self and purpose in life. We can have the most amazing accomplishments and success. We can be very confident in many things we do in life. But if we don't have this synchronicity between our thinking self and are our true, deep self, there will always be a feeling of insecurity that we try in vain to comfort.

Self-esteem is naturally within us. We don't have to do anything to create it. What we need to do is to remove the layers of conditioning that have been smothering our sense of self-worth since childhood. This low self-esteem was embedded in us due to an abnormal childhood environment. Feelings of insecurity followed with fear and pain created a physical and mental state. All the child wanted was to feel safe. They had every right you expect that and when they didn't get it, didn't feel it, it created sensations and ideas of low self-worth which persist through adulthood. These are the layers of conditioning needing cleaning so that the operating system can reboot its natural state.

The process for restoring confidence and self-esteem is this.

1. Spend time in your quiet peaceful self than in your monkey mind. This opens life channels, healing old wounds, and allowing your true nature to rise. The daily program activities give you many opportunities to do exactly this.

2. Becoming more aware of your insecurity allows it to flow. The childhood defense is to shut it down to maintain the mental hold upon it. But allow it to flow and you will notice that it diminishes and releases its hold upon you.

3. As you find yourself becoming more powerful, you'll notice you have new courage for self-discovery and risk-taking. Try new things that excite you. Give yourself credit for trying and for every achievement large and small. It is these actions which will build upon your natural self-esteem and reprogram the negative thinking of low self-esteem. This is a process of noticing your fear and your excitement and continuing to take action for your enjoyment and satisfaction.

How to Live with Damaged Childhood

A damaged childhood is a heavy burden for the adult. Living with abuse or neglect every day every minute for years creates a weak foundation for living life. But it's not what happened to us in childhood but how we responded to it that sets the course of our lives. Many children go through the same situations within the same family but have a completely different response. Some are damaged comma some are not. But no one has to justify or explain their childhood response. Many people make excuses for those that inflicted their torturous childhood environment. One's response is the only thing that matters. The child doesn't have to explain themselves. It doesn't matter who was right or wrong. It doesn't matter how much harm or abuse one had or didn't have. What matters is the child's response. It is the truth and it needs respecting.

And to a child there's one thing that matters above all others. The baby, a toddler, and a child have only one thing they are concerned about. But that one thing is the most powerful force in human nature. It is survival. And if a baby our child of any age feels insecure and their survival is at stake it will generate a number of life strategies to make the bond between them and the caregivers strong and secure. It's not about being loved or loving. The overwhelming desire for a child is safety. And of course this is the way the human species is designed. We don't pop out of the womb ready to run like a deer. We depend upon our caregivers. This is normal. And in this normal environment we grow up feeling loved, confident, and optimistic.

But the damage in childhood occurs when the child does not feel secure. When the survival system is always on high alert due to the persistent stress from insecurity and fear of non-survival. For baby or toddler this fear comes from neglect or not being comforted or touched. This is abnormal. It damages not the childhood, exactly, but the child's survival system itself. The survival system is the strongest human force that's made man the greatest competitor on earth. It is designed to make us bigger, stronger, faster but in this abnormal childhood is transformed into a self-defeating system.

The child can't leave or argue, no they are trapped. What happens then is the physical forces that are generally used to survive are now used to repress. They are needed to repress the pain and fear overwhelming the child to the point of suffocation. This repression of emotions is damaging the child's survival system. But it is the child's final defense in this abnormal situation. And although not their fault, and not the fault of the adult they become, it remains imprinted within them throughout life. But repression and avoidance make for a very unhappy, very alienated adult.

Can we repair this primal, innate system? This root of nearly all dysfunctional adults? We can repair it and not just manage it. Managing implies we're going to use our minds, our thinking, to overcome this repression. That's the biggest myth in therapy. Because this damaged survival system is designed to overpower thinking and willpower under the most stressful conditions. No wonder brilliant people and agile thinkers fail to control self-defeating behaviors. They are using the wrong system, thinking. Sensory-emotional depression and anxiety do not respond to a thinking approach. When the most powerful force in humankind was damaged and used for emotional defense, while the young brain was developing, it's absurd to use thinking to repair it.

We have to use non-think methods to heal this primal system. A sensory approach is required if well-being is to be maintained under stress. The conscious it used to focus upon sensory-emotional objects until new response habits are formed. So, under stress a person doesn't react with obituary childhood responses. They are able to first see their impulses and then use their thinking to apply new actions under stress. In this way the bugs and the malware that had been infecting the operating system since childhood, becoming embedded in the subconscious and automatic human systems, like breathing, will be removed. The need is to repair these sensory systems with conscious, physical procedures. It's not as difficult as it sounds because the original programming is still with in US. It's meditating for mindfulness and living consciously more and more. It's the only method that will transform the damaged childhood system so that it remains strong under stressful life events.

How to live mindfully

Those learning a mindful practice often ask, how can I live mindfully? I can't walk around practicing breathing, focusing, or chanting. I can't live my life while I'm paying attention to my breath. When I'm working my mind is somewhere else. Living mindfully seems as foreign to some as walking on the moon or living like a monk. People want the peace and the clarity they receive from mindful practices, but it seems an impossible jump from mindful practices to their normal, busy lives. The answer to living mindfully is not in how but in what, as in what should I do, not how should it be done.

Mindfulness is a living experience of being connected to one's body and connected even deeper to a higher consciousness. It's experiencing greater awareness of everything we are and everything around us. It requires effort to concentrate on perceptions and sensations while setting aside thoughts and concepts. In this way we become masters of our thinking and thoughts instead of slaves to every whim and idea spinning in the 40,000 or more thoughts we have every day. Mindfulness is a clear learning and living experience rather than an intellectual or intangible one.

The misunderstanding is in the effort required. Mindfulness seems like work. Focusing seems hard. Paying attention needs effort. For people learning a mindfully aware practice, they strain to focus upon the method of the practice. This is because their skill focusing is weak and they find it difficult to maintain for longer periods. This makes focusing one of the five horsemen, critical to living mindfully. Focus requires more than anything else, letting go of all the thinking and thoughts we are attached to. Once we learn to do this it becomes very easy to apply the effort to live consciously. Once we learn to let go our awareness expands and we find ourselves living more mindfully.

Mindfulness is just awareness. It's living consciously. If this is difficult and it is for many, then what are we doing? How are we living? If we're not living consciously then what kind of life is it? We're missing most of the sensations and perceptions which is the fabric of life. Our nourishment and satisfaction in life, which is the reason for life, isn't it. is diminished. Instead of a rich full life we are living a narrow, restricted version of our lives. It's no wonder we feel unfulfilled and dissatisfied. We're playing the chess game of life but it has no heart and soul.

We need to practice mindfulness with methods and techniques, because our busy mind, the Buddhists monkey mind, has this hold upon us day in and day out. As we become better practitioners with more skills our daily life becomes more mindful. We become more connected to everything around us and to our own sensory-emotional flow. Living mindfully requires little effort except for the intention to be more aware and connected. We eat mindfully, our food becomes more pleasurable, and we don't eat to satisfy emotional needs. We walk, clean, and interact with others in a mindfully present attitude, enriching our life and those around us. Is it more difficult to be aware on some level of our simple breath while we're talking to people than to be tightly holding and swallowing and squeezing our breathing instrument? It may seem difficult to do what is simple until we train ourselves for the new normal.

Is it more difficult to be quiet and still than to be anxious and unable to relax? It seems challenging because we've been anxious all our life so we practice to break that pattern until it becomes that new normal, the true experience of self. As you will see in the activities in the daily program, creating true self space is consciously focusing upon an object, breathing being the most common. Who would have thought we have to learn how to be still and quiet? And who would have thought that this would produce so much benefit, so much peace and so much richer life? Living consciously, connected to our sensory-emotional self is so much easier than living blindly, avoiding all that we are, the good, the bad, and the ugly. Is it more pleasurable jumping around in the conditioned monkey mind where thoughts have no weight, where all is impermanent, changing direction from one moment to the next. Mindfulness is the easiest thing in the world, where we find the truth of ourselves.

Reading supplemental and video influencers.

Thich Nhat Hanh, **The Miracle of Mindfulness: An Introduction to the Practice of Meditation**, 1999

Eric Swanson, Yongey Rinpoche Mingyur, **The Joy of Living: Unlocking the Secret and Science of Happiness**, 2007

Soen Nakagawa, **Endless Vow: The Zen Path of Soen Nakagawa**, 1996

Guo Gu, **Passing Through the Gateless Barrier: Koan Practice for Real Life,** 2016

Hiroaki Sato, **The Sword & the Mind: The Classic Japanese Treatise on Swordsmanship and Tactics,** 2004

Kindle Edition

Gabor Maté, The Myth of Normal: Trauma, Illness, and Healing in a Toxic Culture, 2022

Thich Nhat Hanh, **Breathe, You Are Alive: Sutra on the Full Awareness of Breathing Paperback,** 2008

Benson, Herbert, **The Relaxation Response,** New York: William Morrow, 1975

Eckhart Tolle, **The Power of Now: A Guide to Spiritual Enlightenment**, 2010

Chan Master Sheng Yen, **The Method of No-Method: The Chan Practice of Silent Illumination**, 2008

www.ingramcontent.com/pod-product-compliance
Lightning Source LLC
Chambersburg PA
CBHW082041300426
44117CB00015B/2569